CW01500418

Acknowledgements

We would like to thank Sally Campbell for welcoming the idea of a book on Hegel's relevance to Marx when she was at Bookmakers and for commenting on the complete draft. Rhys Williams also read the whole book and provided many detailed comments that helped shape its structure significantly. Thanks to Ken Olende for a very useful discussion on Eurocentrism and for sharing with us an article of his on the subject that was yet to be published. Mark Thomas provided useful comments about the need to make certain sections more accessible. A special mention must go to Richard Donnelly who has been unstintingly enthusiastic throughout the whole project and whose comments and suggestions proved most useful. Finally, thanks to Colm Bryce at Bookmarks for help taking the book from draft form to printed book.

Various audiences, particularly those at Socialist Workers' Party branch meetings, were presented with ideas from the book or at least the distantly related forebears and we would like to thank them for their suggestions.

The painting on the front cover is "Shostakovich" by David Hollington and we are grateful to him for allowing us to use it, as we are to Matt McDowall for photographing the painting. Ben Windsor designed the front cover and the book as a whole and we thank him his efforts.

Preface

Georg Wilhelm Friedrich Hegel is perhaps more than any other mainstream thinker concerned with change. Changing ideas, but also changing material reality — the world we experience everyday. Across the globe workers and peasants have already faced a decade or so of austerity and witnessed a toxic realignment of the right: with fascists part of the government in several European countries and, of course, Donald Trump ensconced in the White House. Given this, change is something that is most definitely needed.

In this short book we have two main aims. The first is to provide an introduction to the thought and life of Hegel to those who are unfamiliar with him. Whilst there are many books and articles on Hegel there are scant few that are accessible to those unfamiliar with philosophy, let alone for those whose chief motivation is not only to understand the world but to change it. We do hope nonetheless that those who are acquainted with Hegel's thought will still find the book of interest, as we offer a new account of at least one important area of his philosophy.

Our second main aim is to outline the very strong influence Hegel had on Karl Marx — the nineteenth-century German revolutionary — and Friedrich Engels, Marx's long-time collaborator, as well the wider Marxist and socialist movement.

Hegel and Revolution

Hegel and Revolution

Terry Sullivan

&

Donny Gluckstein

Hegel and Revolution
by Terry Sullivan and Donny Gluckstein

First published by Bookmarks in 2020

© Bookmarks Publications Ltd
c/o 1 Bloomsbury Street, London WC1B 3QE
www.bookmarksbookshop.co.uk

ISBN 978-1-912926-22-0 paperback
ISBN 978-1-912926-23-7 Kindle
ISBN 978-1-912926-24-4 epub
ISBN 978-1-912926-25-1 pdf

Typeset by Bookmarks Publications
Cover design by Ben Windsor
Printed by Halstan & Co

Contents

This second aim means that there are certain areas of Hegel's thought that we make no reference to as we hold that they had little influence upon Marx and Engels. For example, we make no mention of Hegel's *Lectures on Aesthetics* nor of the *Encyclopaedia of the Philosophical Sciences*. We hope the reader will forgive us for these omissions but appreciate that it makes the fulfilment of our two main aims more achievable.

We will consider three areas of Hegel's thought: his accounts of alienation and dialectics as well as his philosophy of history. Each of these three areas are considered in separate chapters and each chapter will assess just what did Marx learn from Hegel.

In *Chapter 2 — Alienation*, we discuss Hegel's theory of alienation, and offer an account that we argue successfully marries competing explanations. Ludwig Feuerbach's criticism of Hegel's account is considered in some detail before we turn to present Marx's own evaluation. We then examine Marx's criticisms of Feuerbach's account and, in particular, how alienation is to be overcome.

In *Chapter 3 — The Philosophy of History*, we consider the important notions of freedom and, what Hegel calls, spirit. We will argue that more than any other preceding philosopher Hegel placed philosophy, and thought more generally, within an historical context. Although often criticised for the 'idealism' of this thought we show that his approach is much more sophisticated than his critics accept. Much of the chapter is given over to an explanation and critique of three keys notions within Hegel's philosophy of history: the master and slave dialectic, the role of what Hegel calls 'world historical figures' and his notion of the 'cunning of reason'. Finally, we examine Hegel's concept of the state and the so-called 'end of history'.

In *Chapter 4 — Dialectics*, we will examine the structure of Hegel's dialectic, why it has the starting point it does as well as its historical inspirations. We consider what Hegel takes the dialectic to be able to do, as well as trying to correct two misunderstandings concerning it. The contradictory nature of the dialectic is often seen as a fatal flaw but we argue that it is nothing of the sort. However, we do argue that Hegel's account does in fact face two problems that seem insurmountable. Importantly, we make clear the difference between the dialectic of Hegel and that which Marx developed. Finally, we consider Engels' 'laws of dialectics'.

However, before turning to each of these areas it is crucial in order to understand Hegel to place him in his historical context: the crisis of the German Enlightenment in the 1790s, the rise of Romanticism and, most importantly, the aftermath of the French Revolution. This we will do in *Chapter 1 — A Biography of Contradiction*.

Chapter 1
A Biography of Contradiction

It is a paradox typical of his philosophy that Hegel's individual biography illuminates the universality of his thought. He was born in 1770, the son of a civil servant attached to the court of the minor German state of Wurttemberg. He died in 1831 a revered philosophy professor in Berlin, the capital of Prussia, the largest and most powerful German state. Hegel's life spanned a key period in the transition from feudalism to capitalism in Europe. This was one of the most dramatic periods in history and saw enormous change in social, economic and political life.

Hegel not only lived at this time of extraordinary transformation but experienced some of its key events at first hand. For example, he was in Jena in 1806 when Napoleon's forces took control. Some accounts have him crossing the city to the printers with the manuscript of *The Phenomenology of Spirit*,[1] his first mature work, as the battle still raged.

External events are not sufficient in themselves to explain his achievements. Other contemporary philosophers failed to reach the stature of Hegel, and his philosophy certainly cannot be reduced to merely intellectually mirroring events. Nonetheless, the historical backdrop was a substantial influence on his work because through it he sought to comprehend in great depth what was happening. To understand the interconnection between events at the level of society, Hegel's personal biography, and his philosophy, a brief summary of Europe's transition from feudalism to capitalism is necessary.

Land ownership was the economic and political basis of feudal society. The aristocracy directly appropriated the wealth the peasantry generated to reinforce exploitation and defeat rivals (by means of dungeons, castles, armies, and so on). The ideology of the feudal period was encapsulated in the concept of the 'divine right of kings' whose meaning was brilliantly summed up by this German pastor: "God wills that I should obey my superiors. I sin against him if I do not. If I believe myself unjustly treated I may beg them for grace, but I must submit. This is the teaching of Christianity, and the only enlightenment the people needs on its rights".[2] Thus the power of the landowners was sanctified on religious grounds. The Church was a tool used to justify exploitation and domination by the aristocracy.

However, within the bosom of feudalism grew the embryo of a different society. Commerce and the production of commodities for sale did not rest on direct appropriation of agricultural production. So alongside the feudal landowners and aristocrats a new ruling class contender developed — the bourgeoisie with its own economic system — capitalism. In the universities, where Hegel spent most of his adult life, a new way of thinking was promoted. Learning and science were turned into an ideological weapon against feudal obscurantism. The test of Reason was put to war against tradition and blind faith. Freedom from absolutist rule was the watchword, even if the free market would be its ultimate result.

That approach formed the basis for the Enlightenment which blossomed in the middle years of the eighteenth century. Its champions could be found in many countries. They included people like Voltaire and Denis Diderot in France, Adam Smith and David Hume in Britain, Benjamin Franklin in the United

States, and Immanuel Kant and Johann Wolfgang von Goethe in Germany. In the latter country, under conditions of political despotism, exponents of the Enlightenment, (*Aufklarung* in German), attacked feudalism using ideas and blistering critique rather than direct action. Hegel was among their number.

The transition from feudalism to capitalism was a complex phenomenon. It is true that each represented rival social, economic and political systems and so could clash violently. However, they could also co-exist, because what was at stake was not the very existence of exploitation, but which kind of exploitation should be paramount.

The example of Britain is instructive. Here the forces of capitalism broke through successfully (a key moment being the execution of Charles I in 1649). Yet once the new system felt secure a compromise with traditional forces was reached, as symbolised by restoration of the monarchy in 1660. By the late eighteenth century the industrial revolution was dissolving the bonds that held together traditional social structures based on agrarian life. Yet the trappings of feudal society, such as the aristocracy, continued under a constitutional monarchy.

A parallel evolution of conflict followed by compromise occurred in the development of Hegel's social and political attitudes. He emphasised the bourgeoisie's struggle against feudalism early in his life, but in old age reflected its readiness to co-exist with what remained of the previous system. The shift was refracted through the prism of philosophy, in other words at a level of abstraction from immediate circumstances. The result was a profound theoretical framework which transcended the changes from his initial to later views.

Hegel's pattern of youthful advance and elderly retreat can be linked to the country he lived in. Compared to its West European neighbours, the Holy Roman Empire, which included Germany, was a backwater economically and politically, a patchwork of over 300 individual states. His youthful view of his homeland and its *ancien régime* was scathing: "no state has a more wretched constitution than Germany".[3] He concluded that "something must be changed. We must assert this bald truth".[4] Of his native state he wrote: "The whole representative system of Wurttemberg is faulty and in need of thorough-going reform".[5]

Initially he appealed for a return to something like ancient Athens. It was significant that someone who began academic life training to be a priest in the University of Tubingen suggested this pagan society was the ideal model. That expressed Hegel's unease with much of established institutional religion (though not religion itself) and was a common Enlightenment theme. Ignoring the existence of slavery that lay behind it, he believed Greek civilisation deserved admiration because it embodied freedom and self-rule: "As free men they obeyed laws they had given themselves, they obeyed men they had installed in positions of authority, they waged wars they had themselves resolved upon, gave up their property and their passions and sacrificed thousands of lives for a cause that was their own".[6]

Clearly something had brought this ideal world to an end and Hegel explained its decline in these terms:

> The image of the state as a product of his own activity faded from the soul of the citizen; understanding and concern for society as a whole became the province of a single man, or a few men...government of the machine of state was entrusted to a small number of citizens and they served as individual cogs...[7]

This degradation of Greek civilisation was blamed on the Roman Empire that followed the Athenian Golden Age. But it was also a fairly obvious critique of the sorry state of affairs that now obtained in aristocratic Germany, even if the suggested way out depended on a model drawn from a long-lost past.

Hegel's approached changed after the Parisian masses stormed the Bastille in July 1789. In the absolutist state of France, the greatest continental power of Europe, the conflict between feudalism and capitalism had reached its most intense expression. Now instead of having to refer back thousands of years to show the change he desired, he could point to something in the present, and nearby — just over the border from Wurttemberg. Whether the legend of planting a liberty tree in honour of France's revolution during this period is true or not, Hegel saw himself, and the philosophy he propounded, as crucial in promoting this living social experiment. In the 1806 lecture already quoted above, concerning the dissolution of the old world, he went on to say:

A new product of the spirit is being prepared. The chief task of philosophy is to welcome it and grant it recognition, while others, impotently resisting, cling to the past while the majority unconsciously constitute the masses in which it manifests itself.[8]

Admiration for the French Revolution was a view Hegel never departed from. At his fiftieth birthday party in 1820, despite major changes in political outlook since the heady days of his youth, his toast was: "This glass is for the 14th of July 1789 — to the storming of the Bastille".[9] And he was not alone in welcoming the Revolution. To middle class observers everywhere these events seemed to herald the universal triumph of reason and freedom.

However, as the passage from Hegel quoted above makes clear, enthusiasm for the Revolution was shaped by a perspective which was consciously intermediate between the ruling elements of the *ancien régime* and the majority of poor people. The former were 'impotently resisting'; the latter were 'unconsciously' advancing the cause. As an intellectual, Hegel considered himself to be aware of the processes at work, and distinct from either group. Furthermore, with his Enlightenment background he was convinced it was Reason (as expounded by the scientific and rational arguments of progressive thinkers), not the 'mob', which was the motor of change. The source of transformation was therefore to be found in terms of ideas, not the pikestaff.

There can be no doubt of the contempt Hegel had for the

ancien régime. Yet his attitude towards the *sans culottes* — the Parisian masses whose insurrection tore down the walls of the Bastille — was equally dismissive. His conviction was strengthened by the evolution of the Revolution itself.

In the early 1790s radical egalitarian movements in France threatened not only the old ruling class but the wealth and power of the rising bourgeoisie itself. The path of the Revolution did not turn out to be dictated by (middle-class) Reason as many Enlightenment admirers had expected. When the bourgeois dominated National Assembly decided to challenge the King for power it discovered that the power of argument had little effect on the monarch's army. It required the armed women and men of the *sans culottes* to rescue that institution from being forcibly disbanded.

After its salvation the Assembly issued a famous 'Declaration of the Rights of Man'. Its motto 'Liberty, Equality, Fraternity' appeared to benefit all (well all men, at least). The reality was that feudal exploitation was being displaced by capitalist exploitation. The ordinary people of France, and particularly the *sans culottes* of Paris who had saved the day, were expected to meekly accept this arrangement with its new masters. They refused. Having tasted their own power, they strove to drive French society towards true equality, even if that required equality of property and abolition of social hierarchy.

This mass movement from below occurred at the same time as Europe's aristocratic states attacked France, and for a moment the very survival of the Revolution was threatened. Between 1791 and 1793 Robespierre's middle-class Jacobins backed by the Parisian 'mob' saved the day. They overthrew the vacillating Girondins (the party which Hegel supported), centralised power and pioneered wholesale military mobilisation.

The military ardour required to achieve the *levée en masse* — large-scale conscription into vast national armies — relied on ordinary people perceiving the revolution as worth fighting and even dying for. Therefore radical measures such as the Law of Maximum (setting the highest prices that businesses could charge) were enacted. Active supporters of the *ancien régime* were prosecuted, and Christianity uprooted. It seemed that the Revolution could turn against *all* vestiges of privilege and order, and thus against the middle class as well as the aristocrats.

In a striking section of the *Phenomenology of Spirit* clearly referring to the *sans culottes,* Hegel set himself against mass action from below. It reveals that despite his frequent use of the word 'freedom' he saw this as being of a very particular kind. It was freedom for the bourgeoisie, and carefully circumscribed by respect for state law and property.

By contrast those pursuing 'absolute freedom' were putting themselves "on the throne of the world, without any power being able to offer effectual resistance". That was threatening to create a situation where "all social ranks or classes...are effaced and annulled".[10] He regarded this as a deeply negative phenomenon:

> Universal freedom can thus produce neither a positive achievement nor a deed; there is left only negative action; it is merely the rage and fury of destruction... The sole and only work and deed accomplished by universal freedom is therefore death...the most cold-blooded and meaningless death of all.[11]

And yet, despite this hostile judgement of key events in France, Hegel continued to uphold the Revolution vigorously. To accomplish this feat he had to embrace the concept of contradiction.

Hegel's adoption of such a finely-tuned middle approach to the Revolution was not the inevitable result of his membership of the middle class, however. Intellectuals, then and now, can hold views that coincide with the interests of classes very distant from their own social position. In Germany, Fichte, who preceded Hegel as an unsalaried 'Extraordinary Professor' at Jena, strongly identified with the insurgent masses:

The dark ages are over, you people, when you were told in God's name that you were herds of cattle set on earth to fetch and carry, to serve a dozen mortals in high places, and to be their possessions. You are not their property, nor even God's property, but your own. You are stronger than they, for strength is in your arms, as recent events have proved.[12]

At the opposite end, like many early supporters of the French Revolution who later became bitter critics, the philosopher Friedrich Heinrich Jacobi wrote: "My joy in the Revolution ceased in August 1789, and since then I have become ever more hopeless." Soon he was writing: "All Europe must unite against them if it does not want a repetition of its experiences with the Goths, the Huns, and the Vandals".[13] Hegel crossed swords with Jacobi many times.

Hegel's position in the middle proved an advantage. Adhering closely to the core views of the bourgeoisie in the passage from feudalism to capitalism he expressed that all-important outlook very accurately. However, his location in Germany, both next to France but not directly involved in its Revolution, gave him a very particular perspective.

The French Revolution and its aftermath had thrown everything into the melting pot — politics, religion, economics, history, art, and philosophy. Morality, law, and even what constituted reality, were now open to question as never before. The *Phenomenology of Spirit* was published in the seminal year of 1806 and declares: "our epoch is a birth-time, and a period of transition. The spirit of man has broken with the old order of things hitherto prevailing, and with the old ways of thinking".[14] This was not the result of gradual evolution but of a sudden shift of quantity into quality. (For more on such change see Chapter 4). The proceeding process of:

gradual crumbling to pieces, which did not alter the general look and aspect of the whole, [was] interrupted by the sunrise which, in a flash and at a single stroke, brings to view the form and structure of the new world...a widespread revolution in manifold forms of spiritual culture.[15]

Hegel realised that dependence on a single element of the overall picture, or an individual human being, or a piecemeal analysis of separate events, would miss the complex and interconnected character of the transition. "Everything that exists stands in correlation, and this correlation is the veritable nature of every existence".[16] To understand 'existence' itself therefore required a holistic approach which burrowed beneath the chaotic surface appearance and grasped the totality in a coherent manner. As Hegel put it in the *Phenomenology of Spirit*: "The truth is the whole [and] the truth is only realised in the form of system".[17] This approach encompassed all of the natural world and the social world. And, as a child of the Enlightenment, he judged that the whole was discovered through Reason and embodied as thought.

Recognising France's Revolution as the contemporary model for change had other important consequences. Previously, when ancient Greece was in the forefront, his approach had been relatively ahistorical. The glories of the classical age were directly compared to the miserable mediocrity of contemporary Germany. Insofar as the reason for the decline of ancient Greek society was considered, it was to furnish a critique of modern absolutism rather than grasp fundamental patterns of historical development. The French Revolution changed all that.

Firstly, this was not a single event but a complex and developing process. It was ignited by the 'revolt of the nobles' in 1788. A year later came the formation of the middle-class National Assembly, swiftly followed by the sudden intervention of the masses at the Bastille. The government was at its most radical under the Jacobin regime in 1793, while 'Thermidorian Reaction' reversed this in 1794, and so on. Hegel replaced the static juxtaposition of one society (ancient Greece) and contemporary Germany[18] with a lifelong fascination for the dynamics of the historical process.

The driving forces of that totality also had to be reconsidered in the light of French events. During non-revolutionary periods, when people live in relatively static class societies, it can be difficult for them to feel more than passive bystanders, the object of developments beyond their control. The fall of the Bastille showed that human beings could collectively transform history. Bringing about change did not have to be the exclusive privilege of kings and queens. However, Hegel, as a middle class intellectual, looked down on the masses, regarding them as the blind tool of other forces.

So for him, while massive and dramatic events were taking place, this must be the work of abstract ideas rather than real people. Hegel's approach coincided with a bourgeois perspective on current events. The inspiring slogan of the French Republic, 'Liberty, Equality and Fraternity', (to which Hegel as a child of the Enlightenment would have added 'Reason'), dare not be conceived in prosaic terms such as 'freedom to exploit', or 'equal opportunity to make profit', and so on. It had to be ennobled, appearing as a great idea equally valid for the masses and the budding capitalist class. The former would not storm the citadels of aristocratic power merely to increase the profits of rich businessmen. Thus the dawn of the bourgeois age had to be envisaged as being of universal benefit rather than grubby class interest, as an abstract concept rather than material reality.

Despite his mystification of the process, the French Revolution had opened up avenues for a major advance in Hegel's thinking. Its evolution continued to drive him forward. By 1794 the ascendancy of the French bourgeoisie was secure. The masses had swept away feudal society and swelled the ranks of the victorious revolutionary armies. That year they were neutralised — set to work as objects of exploitation or to serve as cannon fodder for French imperial expansion. The figurehead for this overall process of bourgeois consolidation was

Napoleon, who proclaimed himself Emperor in 1802. Many advanced thinkers, such as Beethoven, were disgusted by his self-coronation. Yet to Hegel the modern world now had the equivalent of Theseus, the legendary leader of the Athenians. Instead of 'absolute freedom and terror' France, and soon much of Europe, would be under 'the rule of law' rather than the arbitrary whim of absolutist monarchs or the dangerous masses.[19]

In 1806 Hegel saw Napoleon in action at Jena when his army dealt a crushing blow to France's enemies. Within thirteen days of the Battle of Jena French soldiers were in Berlin. Hegel's reaction to this event was the very opposite of nationalistic. He wrote: "I saw the Emperor — this world soul riding out of the city...It is indeed a wonderful sensation to see such an individual, who, concentrated here at a single point, astride a horse, reaches out over the world and masters it".[20] Rather than considering Napoleon's conquest a tragedy for his own country he suggested that it would "affect internal organisation too, to the advantage of the peoples".[21] For Hegel, Napoleon's achievement was simultaneously that of an individual and the expression of the wider Revolution. This is the meaning of the term 'world soul'.[22] It combined both universal and individual notions. Napoleon was taken to embody the establishment of bourgeois (as opposed to 'absolute' or human) freedom, secured from above by the actions of a dictator.

However, in 1813 the Emperor's forces were routed and two years later the Bourbon monarchy was restored in France. Although the social and economic basis of feudalism was beyond repair, political Reaction was firmly in the saddle across the Confederation of German states, leading to measures such as the infamous Carlsbad Decrees. These bore down on freedom of speech and put supporters of the revolution at risk of arrest. At this time Hegel had moved to Prussia which was one of the most repressive German states. Renowned philosopher he may have been, but he was still clearly at risk since close associates were jailed or driven into exile for subversion or atheism. The poet Heine was a personal student and judged that Hegel wrote: "in very obscure and abstruse signs so that not everyone could decipher them — I sometimes saw him anxiously looking over his shoulder, for fear that he had been understood...".[23] In 1819 Hegel wrote to a friend: "I am about to be fifty years old, and I have spent thirty of these fifty years in these eternally uneasy times of fear and hope. I had hoped that for once we might be done with it. Now I see that things... are getting ever worse".[24]

The consequences were soon to be clear. In his youth Hegel wanted philosophy to change the world, writing in 1808: "I become more convinced every day that theoretical work accomplishes more than practical. Once the realm of ideas has been revolutionised, reality cannot hold out".[25] By 1820 his view of philosophy's role had reversed. Surrounded by Reaction he felt reality had held out after all. It was therefore safer to claim philosophy only interpreted things *after the event*. Referring to the symbol of the Roman Goddess of Wisdom he wrote in 1820 that thought: "appears only when actuality has completed the process of formation and attained its finished state... The owl of Minerva begins its flight only with the falling of dusk".[26] Restoration in France and Reaction at home had led to more than personal disquiet. It coincided with a general loss of nerve in the German middle class, one which was to endure for decades.

In these circumstances Hegel began to turn to the very political force that he had earlier seen as an obstacle to progress — Germany's political structures and the Prussian state in particular. The French threat to Prussia had indeed forced it to begin modernisation to better match its enemy. From 1807 the Stein-Hardenburg reforms led to more efficient administration, and serfdom was abolished. But undertaking reforms to better preserve the old establishment was a complicated affair. The co-existence of remnants of the past society with elements of modern bourgeois society was highly contradictory. The ruling aristocracy in Prussia had adopted some modern bourgeois methods to maintain its monopoly of state power. This meant the middle class could prosper even though they were denied political progress.

Hegel now put this situation into philosophical form. The bridge across which he transitioned, apparently seamlessly, from radical to reactionary was described in a famous and splendidly ambiguous phrase from his Preface to *The Philosophy of Right*. It has been translated in various ways, one variant being: "What is real is rational, and what is rational is real".[27] A youthful radical reading would affirm that what exists must be made to conform to the demands of Reason, the French Revolution being a means of compelling this to happen. The reactionary interpretation he made in later years justified the situation in Germany after Waterloo: what existed already conformed to Reason and on those grounds dare not be challenged.

The insights he had gained from the French Revolution regarding historical development, the importance of understanding the totality and the contradictory relationships it contained — in sum the understanding of dialectics that he had achieved — were not lost. They could now be turned to analyse this new and complex situation. The method remained the same, as did the class perspective. What changed was the political content, because opposition to the *status quo* had been converted into promotion of it.

The new direction could be seen in a number of ways. Instead of praising the transformative effect of the French Revolution Hegel began to emphasise the Protestant Reformation that began in Germany back in 1517. The Catholicism of France, he asserted, led to political servitude before 1789 and the dangerously explosive character of the French events that followed: "For it is a false principle that the shackles which bind right and freedom can be broken without the emancipation of the conscience, that there can be a Revolution without a Reformation".[28] Having geographically relocated the model to be admired northwards (from France to Germany), he called for obedience to its rule: "there is no point in asking how the state was formed, was it out of patriarchal concern, out of corporations, out of fear, these are just external appearances. The right of the state derives from its having rational authority".[29]

Hegel was also prepared to simply re-write the order of events to suit his current purpose. No longer was it true that Germany had had the most 'wretched constitution'. For even before the French Revolution: "In Germany the entire compass of secular relations had already undergone a change for the better".[30] If this had not borne fruit hitherto that was because it was too mixed up with negative features. The latter had now filtered out as a result of Napoleon's intervention. "French oppression was the especial means of bringing to light the deficiencies of the old system." As a result: "Feudal obligations are abolished, for freedom of property and of person have been recognised as fundamental principles...".[31]

Now that economic barriers to the development of capitalism were removed, Hegel also concluded that there was no need to worry about the remnants of feudalism or to unleash dangerous radical forces to remove them. The scandal of rule by 'a single man, or a few men' was no longer a concern: "the sole arbitration of the monarch is, in point of substance, no great matter... Those who know ought to govern — not ignorance and the presumptuous conceit of 'knowing better'".[32]

Superficially regarded, one could easily slip into thinking that as Hegel grew older he entirely lost touch with his radical roots, and that his stance was incoherent or inconsistent. Many have thought so. Terry Pinkard, who has written probably the best English biography available, tries to defend Hegel by suggesting that he was "unfairly criticised both during and after [his] lifetime..."[33] for holding reactionary views.

Both criticism and defence are mistaken. Two elements subsisted as a constant within his mature philosophy — a sharp and all-embracing analysis of revolutionary change in all its rich complexity, and the use of this analysis to address very specific concerns of the middle class at the time. Whether in youth or old age neither Hegel's philosophical approach, nor his approach as a member of the middle class, changed in their essentials even if the conclusions he drew were almost diametrically opposed.

What did change was the position of the middle class. Before 1789 many of its members had been fiercely critical of the *status quo.* Now, after the French Revolution, in some places it was the established ruling class, and in others, such as Germany, it was gradually becoming so, sometimes by combining with the old ruling class (what Bismarck would later call 'the marriage of iron and rye'). The process was not necessarily smooth and there were bumps along the way (such as the 1848 revolution, dissolution of the bourgeois Frankfurt Parliament that it produced and so on). Nevertheless, to be consistent the erstwhile critic of the pre-1789 *status quo* must become the defender of the post-1789 *status quo*, and there was no fiercer defender than Hegel.

In conclusion — the strength of Hegel's legacy is that it was rooted in the momentous transition from feudalism to capitalism that reached its apogee in the French Revolution. This specificity should not be regarded as a factor limiting the validity of his thought beyond that period. Indeed, the reverse is true. As might be said of great artists such as Shakespeare, the very degree to which their art reflects the reality of the situation in which they find themselves means that it transcends the time of its creation, while remaining true to that period. Only by understanding both the philosophy and the soil from which it grew can a proper appreciation of Hegel's importance be achieved.

Chapter 2
Alienation

Most people now live in towns and cities that are larger and more densely populated than ever before in human history yet our lives seem to be increasingly dominated by feelings of loneliness. Through the internet we can instantly communicate with billions of other people but many of us seem to be increasingly isolated. The feeling that you have little or no connection with the people and world around you is known as alienation. This is clearly not how one would wish the world to be. But is it an inevitable consequence of contemporary society?

One reason to try and get to grips with what Hegel has to say about such feelings of alienation is that he was one of the very first thinkers to develop such a theory. A second reason is that his thought has had a very important impact on the current understanding of alienation. Matters here will unfortunately not be straightforward at all, not least because Hegel's theory involves one of the most difficult concepts in the whole of philosophy – namely, his account of what he calls 'spirit'. However, we would ask for the readers' perseverance because ultimately, or so we will argue, it will allow us to address of one of the most central questions facing humanity: namely, how can we overcome the feelings of isolation and loneliness that characterise contempory capitalism?

Hegel was one of the very first thinkers to develop a theory of alienation and his most important discussion takes place in the *Phenomenology of Spirit*. Phenomenology is the study of consciousness and its possible structures as experienced from the first-person point of view. It is important for Hegel because he believes, as we shall argue in *Chapter 4 — Dialectics*, that science holds that we should not accept something as true simply because someone says that it is. Rather he argues that one should "examine everything for oneself and follow only one's own conviction, or better still, to produce everything oneself, and accept only one's own deeds".[34]

Given that Hegel holds that we should examine everything, then the place to start is in our thoughts about the world, our starting point should be the study of consciousness — this study being phenomenology. This ties into the Enlightenment concept of 'reason' as distinct from the medieval religious outlook. However, importantly for Hegel consciousness is not just the consciousness of the individual but it is also the consciousness of spirit.[35] More precisely this should be 'Absolute Spirit', that is, God. This might lead the reader to question: 'How does this square with the first-person point of view of phenomenology?' Hegel rejected the common idea that God is different from and superior to the world it has created. Rather, he held that God is in some sense constituted by humans and the natural world. Consequently, humans including the self-examination of their consciousness that, make up, at least in part, God. (For a much fuller discussion on these ideas see Chapter 3.)

Hegel's Alienation

Hegel's theory of alienation concerns the spirit, the separation of the object of the spirit and the subject of the spirit. 'Object' refers to a person or thing to which a specified action or feeling is directed. Put another way, the object is the target of an action. 'Subject' refers to a person or thing which brings about the directed action. Or, to express this differently, that acts upon the world. Hegel's general description of alienation is given by the following quote from the section of the *Phenomenology of Spirit* entitled *Self-alienated spirit: Culture:*

> ...the spirit whose self is an absolutely discrete unit has its content confronting it as an equally hard unyielding reality, and here the world has the character of being something external, the negative of self-consciousness. This world is, however, a spiritual entity, it is in itself the interfusion of being and individuality; this its exist- ence is the *work* of self-consciousness, but it is also an alien reality already present and given, a reality which has a being of its own and in which it does not recog- nize [sic] itself.[36]

It seems clear here that the general sense of alienation is that the spirit (the subject) experiences its own actions (the object) as something external to itself. As Hegel states "the world has the character of being something external". We will argue that this sense of something being external, or alienated, has four facets. One is that the spirit is unable to see that it is in fact the agent that has created the state of affairs, that is, the world. As Hegel writes, the world "is the *work* of the self-consciousness". The second is that although it itself creates the actual world through its labour it is not aware of this. He argues the self-consciousness "does not recognize itself". The third facet is that as a consequence of not recognising that it is the creator of the world, the world appears to it as something given and so beyond its control. Hegel notes, the world appears as "alien reality already present and given, a reality which has a being of its own". Further, and this is the fourth facet, since the world appears as a given it seems to act upon the self-consciousness rather than self-consciousness acting on the world. As he claims, only slightly later in the *Phenomenology of Spirit*, the world "seems to inflict on self-consciousness from without".[37]

A number of writers including Richard Norman and Charles

Taylor[38] have given a different account of Hegel's theory of alienation. For them alienation is the separation, in some way, of the individual and society. This is an important point to note as this seems to fit well with our everyday use of the term 'alienation'. Norman argues, for Hegel "This is alienation as a relation of the individual to the social world".[39] Taylor elaborates his view of the relation as follows: "The happiest, unalienated life for man, which the Greeks enjoyed, is where the norms and ends expressed in the public life of a society are the most important ones by which its members define their identity as human beings".[40] Taylor correctly argues that there is a real sense in which it is impossible, at least totally, to evade the influence of the institutions of public life upon our own individual thoughts and actions. These institutions are the essence or 'substance' of the self and individuals do not feel that these institutions are alien to themselves. And, as Hegel himself writes, "In the universal spirit, therefore, each has only the certainty of himself, of finding in the actual world nothing but himself; he is as certain of others as he is of himself".[41] Taylor's conclusion is that "To live in a state of this kind is to be free".[42]

According to Taylor "alienation arises when the goals, norms or ends which define common practices or institutions begin to seem irrelevant or even monstrous, or when the norms are redefined so that the practices appear a travesty of them".[43] Writing nearly forty years ago he gives the example of Spain, which although it was and still officially is a Catholic country has a large proportion of its population that is strongly anti-clerical. One may argue about the situation in Spain but Taylor's point is clear enough. Further, when people are alienated they have to turn elsewhere in order to define what is centrally important to them. One possibility, which Hegel saw as having great historical importance, is that people try to establish their identity as individuals. The individual ceases to define their identity principally by their public experience of society. On the contrary, the most meaningful experience, which seems to them most vital, is private. However, the public still remains important to some extent. Further, we now have two centres of where the individual can define who they are and this gives rise to the possibility of conflict between them and, subsequently, of alienation.

One challenge to Norman's and Taylor's account of alienation as a relation between individual and society is that it is mistaken to hold that the Greek epoch was an example of an unalienated life. As we shall elaborate in *Chapter 3 — The Philosophy of History*, in the Greek epoch only some were free, the freemen, whilst slaves were not. However, it seems to us that seeking to pit the two accounts of alienation we have discussed against one another may itself be mistaken. This is because there appears to be third way to understand Hegel's theory that in fact marries these two accounts.

To appreciate why this third way may in fact be the correct manner to understand Hegel's theory of alienation it is important to be aware that Hegel was writing shortly after the death of Kant. Kant was a towering figure in German thought and is widely seen as the greatest Western philosopher since the ancient Greek Aristotle. Kant falsely argued that we cannot know reality, what he calls the thing-in-itself, rather we can only know the appearance of reality. Hegel quite rightly rejects this and goes on to argue that we can actually know the world with certainty. Throughout the *Phenomenology of Spirit*, and in a number of other works, Hegel writes of a consciousness 'being-in-itself' and also 'being-for-itself'. By 'in-itself' he is referring to what he calls a thing's 'intrinsic nature'. (As he himself writes, "*in-itself* or *intrinsic* nature".[44]) Perhaps the best way to understand the concept of 'in-itself' is that something constitutes an object in an ordinary sense, that is, as argued above, it is a consciousness to which a specified action or feeling is directed or is the target of an action. According to Hegel, being-for-itself equates to the will, it is what makes something a subject, something that acts upon the world. (Again, as Hegel writes, "The *being-for-itself*, the *will*".[45]) On this account alienation occurs when being-in-itself becomes separated from being-for-itself. As Hegel puts it "self-alienated, being-for-itself is separated from being-in-itself".[46]

Hegel also employs the phrase 'being-in-and-for-itself'. This is where the intrinsic nature of consciousness — the object — is re-united with the will of consciousness — the subject. So, when a consciousness is being-in-itself *and* being-for-itself this is another way of saying that the alienation of the object and subject of spirit has been overcome. At the same time, as we have seen, humans can find certainty in the universal spirit because they can find all of their goals, norms or ends defined in common practices (which in turn are created by individuals). Where this is the case there is a unity of the individual and the wider world.

No doubt not all will agree with our account. One reason may be that they hold that Hegel locates the source of aliena-tion elsewhere. For example, none less than Engels himself, writing in *Ludwig Feuerbach and the End of Classical German Philosophy*, argues that "nature in the Hegelian system repre-sents merely the 'alienation' of the absolute idea".[47] However, one virtue of our above marrying is that it seems to combine the various aspects of Hegel's account of alienation into a more-or-less coherent whole. A second reason to accept that Hegel's account involved a separation between not only subject and object, as well as consciousness and self-consciousness, but 'being-in-itself' and 'being-for-itself' is that this very point seems to be suggested by Marx. Writing in the 'Critique of the Hegelian Dialectic and Philosophy as a Whole', which appears in the *Economic and Philosophic Manuscripts of 1844*, Marx argues that: "The *estrangement*, which therefore forms the real interest of this alienation and of the transcendence of this alienation, is the opposition of *in itself* and *for itself*, of *consciousness* and *self-consciousness*, of *object* and *subject*." He continues that: "All other oppositions and movements of these oppositions are but the *semblance, the cloak, the exoteric* shape of these oppositions which alone matter, and which constitute the *meaning* of these other, profane oppositions".[48]

Above, we rejected Taylor's claims that during the Greek

epoch humans were able to lead an unalienated life. However, Hegel does hold that alienation will come to an end. If our account is correct, then this will occur when object and subject of the spirit are united, when all individuals see the goals, norms or ends which define common practices or institutions as their very own and, finally, when consciousness being is both 'being in-itself' and 'being for-itself'.

Hegel had a very clear idea of when and where this would take place: namely, during the Germanic epoch in what is modern day Germany, since this is, as we shall argue in *Chapter 3 — The Philosophy of History*, when Hegel holds history will end. He writes that the mind:

> Grasps the principle of the unity of the divine nature and the human, the reconciliation of objective truth and freedom as truth and freedom appearing within self-consciousness and subjectivity, a reconciliation with the fulfilment of which, the principle of the Germanic peoples, has been entrusted.[49]

Feuerbach's Criticism of Hegel

It was not long after his death in 1831 that Hegel's account of alienation faced its most damaging criticism. As Frederick Beiser notes "The publication of Feuerbach's *Das Wesen des Christenhums* [*The Essence of Christianity*] in 1841 convinced many of the need to go beyond Hegel".[50]

As noted at the start of this chapter, Hegel held that God is made up by humans and the natural world. He rejected the more common idea that God differs from and is superior to the world it has created. Further, he held that God becomes only fully aware of itself when we humans are fully conscious of God. However, as Feuerbach argues:

> But if it is only in human feelings and wants that the divine 'nothing' becomes something, obtains qualities, then the being of man is alone the real being of God,

— man is the real God. And if in the consciousness which man has of God first arises the self-consciousness of God, then the human consciousness is, *per se*, the divine consciousnesses.[51]

In short, God is not so much dead as superfluous. Feuerbach goes on to ask of Hegel "Why then dost thou alienate man's consciousness from him, and make it the self-consciousness of a being distinct from man, of that which is an object to him".[52] That is, Feuerbach is rightly critical of Hegel's account of a god becoming aware of itself, for this is not the end of alienation, rather the very positing of a god (of something distinct from human beings) is in fact the source of alienation. "The true statement is this," Feuerbach continues "man's knowledge of God is man's knowledge of himself, of his own nature. Only the unity of being and consciousness is truth".[53]

Thus, according to Feuerbach, Hegel's account is standing on its head — to use Marx's phrase, and he placed it right side up.[54] Humans are recognised as the actually existing subject and God is seen as a mere phantom of our minds.

This, argued Feuerbach, is at the core of not only Christianity but all religions that posit gods. Religions take human powers, the ability to think about and act on the world, and project them onto an imaginary being or beings.

These human powers then become alien from us and it is gods — the products of human thoughts — who supposedly have the knowledge of the world and the ability to change it. These human powers somehow become wildly enhanced in the name of religion so that gods are often depicted as being all-powerful, all-knowing and/or existing everywhere. Meanwhile most, though not all, humans are often devalued and regarded as weak or sinful, the puppets of their own inventions. In short, they are alienated from their very human powers.

Feuerbach's writings had a profound effect upon Marx and Engels. Engels writing in *Ludwig Feuerbach and the End of German Classical Philosophy*, argued that Feuerbach had:

placed materialism on the throne again. Nature exists independently of all philosophy. It is the foundation upon which we human beings, ourselves products of nature, have grown up. Nothing exists outside nature and man, and the higher beings our religious fantasies have created are only the fantastic reflections of our own essence... One must have experienced the liberating effect of this book to get an idea of it. Enthusiasm was general; *we all became at once Feuerbachians.*[55]

Further, Marx's criticisms of Hegel's account of alienation (see below) builds upon the above Feuerbachian critique. This is not to say that Marx and Engels were uncritical of Feuerbach's account, Marx's *Theses on Feuerbach* being testament to this.[56]

Marx — Hegel's Double Error

Before proceeding to Marx's powerful criticisms of Hegel's account of alienation it is important to note that Marx holds the account to be one of the great achievements of the *Phenomenology of Spirit*. "The outstanding thing in Hegel's *Phenomenology* and its final outcome...is thus first that Hegel...conceives objectification as loss of the object, as alienation".[57]

Writing in 'Critique of the Hegelian Dialectic and Philosophy as a Whole' Marx argues that "There is a double error in Hegel".[58] The first is that "When, for instance, wealth, state-power, etc., are understood by Hegel as entities estranged from the *human* being, this only happens in their form as thoughts".[59] That is, for Hegel it is not wealth (or the lack of it), state-power or anything else that we experience as part of the material reality of our lives that is of primary importance in understanding alienation. It is not our separation from and lack of control over these aspects of the material world that is the source of our alienation. Rather, it is the thought of such entities which confronts us as something alien.

The second part of the double error Marx argued befell Hegel's account of alienation is that "The only labour which Hegel knows and recognizes is *abstractly mental* labour".[60] Consequently, it is only the mind that is the true essence of humans, not the sensuous material reality of the world around us. The all-important upshot then of Hegel's double error of seeing alienation as thoughts confronting us as alien and that all labour is mental labour, is that the overcoming of alienation is nothing but the movement or changing of thoughts. In short, for Hegel the overcoming of alienation takes place as a change of mind.

Having outlined the double error that Marx argued Hegel made in understanding alienation we now turn to consideration of both how Marx's account differed from Hegel's and what it shared. We have argued that for Hegel one aspect of alienation is when there are two spheres in which individuals can define who they are: the wider community or state, and the private realm. Hegel argues that, putting things simply, the first is 'Good', the second is 'Bad', but immediately goes on to claim — without argument — that the essence of the first is 'state power', the second wealth. Hegel next argues that:

> As state power is the simple substance, so too is it the universal 'work' — the absolute 'heart of the matter' itself in which individuals find their essential nature expressed, and where their separate individuality is merely a consciousness of their universality. It is also the 'work' and the simple *result* from which the sense that it results from *their doing* has vanished; it remains the absolute foundation and subsistence of all that they do.[61]

It is clear here that according to Hegel humans express their essential or fundamental nature through the state. Further, we would also argue that here Hegel is asserting that the source of our alienation is the fact that we are unaware that the result of our own doing, the human-made world around us, is actually made by us. Put another way, we humans have created the world around us but we are not aware of this and thus we are alienated from it.

The first point to make is that for Marx state power is not the locus of alienation. To see this, consider that for Marx the need to labour on nature to satisfy human needs was the only consistent feature of all human societies, the everlasting nature-imposed condition of the human existence. As Marx (and Engels) note in *The German Ideology*:

> [T]he first premise of all human existence and, therefore, of all history, the premise, namely, that men must be in a position to live in order to be able to "make history". But life involves before everything else eating and drinking, a habitation, clothing and many other things. The first historical act is thus the production of the means to satisfy these needs, the production of material life itself.[62]

Thus, for Marx and Engels work — not state power — is the very foundation of all that we do. When Hegel claimed that through the state we find our "essential nature expressed", Marx argued that our capacity for conscious labouring is our 'species being'. Where "the productive life is the life of the species... The whole character of a species — its species character — is outlined in the character of its life-activity; and free, conscious activity is man's species character".[63] However, there is some commonality between Hegel and Marx's account. To see this consider that in the *Economic and Philosophic Manuscripts of 1844* Marx asserts that the alienation of man (and woman) stems from the fact "that his labo[u]r becomes an object, an *external* existence, but that it exists *outside him*, independently, as confronting him; it means that the life which he has conferred on the object confronts him as something hostile and alien".[64] The key notion here for Marx, echoing Hegel, is externality. As Marx asserts, in answer to the question: what constitutes alienation?, it is "the fact that labor is *external* to the worker".[65] Alienation is, in other words, the loss of control over our labour.

The *Theses on Feuerbach*

We noted the profound effect Feuerbach's writings had on Marx and Engels, which helped Marx build upon in his own critique of Hegel's theory of alienation. However, Marx was also critical of Feuerbach himself. As we have seen, Feuerbach correctly argued that the ideas people have are the result of material reality. However, he argued that alienation was not to be overcome by changing this material reality but rather by changing the ideas that people had in their heads. Further, he proposed to change these ideas by educating people to live differently, free from the influence of religion. Marx argued that this was fundamentally inadequate.

Part of the source of Feuerbach's limitation was that he held human nature to be fixed. In rejecting Hegel's idealism he also rejected the dynamism of Hegel's thought — here, the key notion is that human societies change and new forms of organisation can arise. Marx and Engels aptly summed up Feuerbach's position when they wrote that "As far as Feuerbach is a materialist he does not deal with history, and as far as he considers history he is not a materialist".[66] Marx, on the other hand, did not reject the dynamism of Hegel's thought. Marx held that as the way in which society was structured changed, so did how humans behaved and interacted. Crucial here is how work or labour is organised. This meant that if humans wish to fight to overcome alienation they must do so by changing how the material world, and in particular work, is ordered. Trying to change the ideas in people's heads would be futile unless the material reality in which they live and work is not also simultaneously changed. As Marx writes in the third of his thesis on Feuerbach:

> The materialist doctrine that men are the products of circumstances and upbringing, and that, therefore, changed men are the products of other circumstances, forgets that it is men who change circumstances and that it is essential to educate the educator himself. Hence, this doctrine necessarily arrives at dividing society into

two parts, one of which is superior to society.

The coincidence of the changing of circumstances and of human activity or self-changing can be conceived and rationally understood only as *revolutionary practice*.[67]

The two key points to stress here are that first, changing people's ideas requires transforming the circumstances in which they live and work. The second is that this change requires revolutionary practice or the act of fundamentally changing the material world. These two points lie at the very heart of Marx's thought and Marxism more generally. And it is in light of this that Marx declares in the eleventh thesis on Feuerbach that "The philosophers have only *interpreted* the world, in various ways; the point, however, is to *change* it".[68]

A 'Class-in-Itself' and a 'Class-for-Itself'

We have seen above how Hegel distinguishes between consciousness 'being-in-itself' and also 'being-for-itself' and this is the last way in which we will point out how Hegel's account of alienation influences Marx. Some readers may be aware of a distinction in Marxist thought between a 'class-in-itself' and a 'class-for-itself'. The notion of a class in-itself refers to whether a group objectively forms a class, that is, our objective place in the network of ownership and control. A class-for-itself refers to the attitudes or class consciousness of this group and whether they recognise that they share a common interest and moreover are able and prepared to act in this interest. With this distinction made, it is clear that although a class may exist it may not be actually acting in its own interests or only acting minimally in this way. This is an important theoretical tool to help us understand the level and character of class struggle. It helps us realise that even, as at the present moment, when working class people face real and massive attacks through austerity and attempts to divide us though racism and the scapegoating of refugees, there may be little resistance. One reason that workers may not recognise, and consequently not collectively fight these attacks, is because they do not recognise or only partially recognise that *all* workers face these attacks and they collectively have the power to defeat them. This distinction is of much importance for Marx and Marxists more generally as a vital tool in understanding why low levels of class consciousness and resistance occur.

What is perhaps surprising is that Marx never actually uses the terminology 'class-in-itself' (although he does use 'class for itself'). This has led some, most notably Edward Andrew, to argue that "Marx never referred to classes in themselves or distinguished a class in itself from a class for itself".[69] Whilst it is curious to note that Marx never used the phrase 'class-in-itself', Andrew and others are fundamentally mistaken to draw the conclusion that Marx never made the distinction between it and a 'class-for-itself'. To see this, consider the following quote from Marx in *The Poverty of Philosophy*:

> Economic conditions had first transformed the mass of the people of the country into workers. The combination of capital has created for this mass a common situation, common interests. This mass is thus already a class as against capital but not yet for itself. In the struggle, of which we have noted only a few phases, this mass becomes united, and constitutes itself as a class for itself. The interests it defends become class interests. But the struggle of class against class is a political struggle.[70]

Here Marx uses the phrase 'class for itself' and it is clear that for him a class is a class for itself when it is united and defends or fights for its own interests. Although Marx does not use the phrase 'class in itself' he does talk of "a class as against capital". This class as against capital was formed by economic conditions that turned people into workers sharing a common situation who were not capitalists. This account clearly refers to whether a group objectively forms a class, that is, a group's objective place in the network of ownership and control, in other words it refers to a class in-itself.

Lukács On Alienation

Georg Lukács was probably the most influential Marxist thinker on alienation after Marx himself and it would be remiss of us not to consider his account of alienation in Hegel, albeit briefly. In *The Young Hegel* Lukács argues that there is a "specifically capitalist form of 'alienation', i.e., what Marx would later call 'fetishism'".[71] Lukács acknowledges that "Hegel has no clear insight into what is involved here" but insists that Hegel "undoubtedly has intimations of the problems arising from the fetishization of objects in capitalist society" and concludes that "there are undoubtedly powerful tendencies in Hegel to explain the fetishized objectivity of socio-economic formations in terms of the social relations between men".[72]

Fetishism, Marx argued, is the fact that in capitalist societies material objects have certain characteristics conferred on them in virtue of the existing social relations. Further, material objects take on the appearance that such characteristics belong to them not as the result of social relations but rather are in their nature. An example might be the belief that money, when it is invested, somehow increases its own value. Marx uses the analogy of religion, in which, as we have seen, people may bestow imaginary powers upon a fictitious entity, a god. This analogy is not exact, for the characteristics bestowed on material objects under capitalism are real and, unlike religion, not the product of our imaginations. However, neither are they natural characteristics; rather, they are social. And although these characteristics constitute real powers they are not controlled by humans; in fact they hold sway over us.

Unfortunately, Lukács does not quote from Hegel or refer to specifically where such intimations or tendencies concerning fetishism take place. Given this it is not possible to assess whether Lukács is in fact right and whether there are in fact tendencies in Hegel to explain fetishism.

What did Marx Learn from Hegel?

In conclusion, Marx learnt three things from Hegel's account of alienation. The first is that alienation must be placed at the very heart of our understanding of the world. The second is that alienation is the result of something, for Marx labour, that is external to us. The third is that Marx uses Hegel's distinction between consciousness 'being-in-itself' and also 'being-for-itself' to distinguish between a 'class-in-itself' — whether a group objectively forms a class — and the class consciousness of this group.

However, there is one more area where Marx appears to have been directly influenced by Hegel. He also held that alienation would, or rather could, come to an end. For Hegel this occurs when history comes to an end and all humans are free. We can now see that this freedom is a freedom from alienation.[1] For Marx the alienation of humans stems from the fact "the object which labour produces — labour's product — confronts it as *something alien*, as a *power independent* of the producer".[73] However, for Marx alienation ends not with Protestantism and the German state but with the end of class society, with communism, where communism is:

> [T]he *positive* transcendence of *private* property, or *human self-estrangement*, and therefore as the real appropriation of the human essence by and for man; communism therefore as the real *appropriation of the human essence* by and for man; communism therefore as the complete return of man to himself as a social (i.e., human) being — a return become conscious, and accomplished within the entire wealth of previous

1 This is not to say that freedom from alienation is all that freedom amounts to. The freedom to think and the freedom to act, spring to mind for instance. Thus, the freedom from alienation may be seen as a perquisite for these other freedoms to be exercised.

development. This communism, as fully developed humanism, equals naturalism; it is the *genuine* resolution of the conflict between man and nature and between man and man — the true resolution of the strife between existence and essence, between objectification and self-confirmation, between freedom and necessity, between the individual and the species. Communism is the riddle of history solved, and it knows itself to this solution.[74]

Communism is the riddle of history solved because it is the end of alienation.

Chapter 3
The Philosophy of History

A great many Western philosophers before Hegel saw the world as fundamentally unchanging,[75] and their role as being to reveal universal truths about it. In contrast, Hegel was resolute in his belief that everything had a history. Further, the job of philosophers was not only to insist upon the importance of historical context but also to understand the processes that drive historical change.

As we have mentioned, understanding Hegel can be tricky and Hegel's philosophy of history is no exception. At first this might seem somewhat odd as Hegel very obligingly delivered a series of lectures on the philosophy of history that Eduard Gans edited into a book bearing that title.[76]

Unfortunately this work is largely not concerned with the philosophy of history but rather history itself, presenting a grand sweep of what Hegel calls the 'Oriental', 'Greek', 'Roman' and 'Germanic' worlds. Yet in *Lectures on the Philosophy of World History — Introduction: Reason in History* his philosophy of history is outlined.[77] This work is widely referred to as *Introduction* and we shall follow this tradition. A particular challenge with understanding Hegel's philosophy of history is that this work is an "impure text".[78] These lectures were compiled partly from Hegel's own manuscripts and partly from manuscripts made by students. Further, no fewer than four editors have worked at the task of trying to bring this material into a coherent whole. (The philosophy of history is not alone here, similar situations hold with regard to his thinking about aesthetics, the philosophy of religion and the history of philosophy.)

One final point to be made by way of introduction is that Hegel is both concerned with history — that is, the *study* of events and processes that have happened, and with the things that have happened themselves. It is the latter which will be our focus because it is this that has had the greater impact on the thought of Marx and others.

Freedom, Spirit and God

As we have seen above spirit is a term of rich significance for Hegel. For our present purposes it is important to stress that whilst he acknowledges that "Physical nature also plays a part in world history...the spirit and the course of its development are the true substance of history",[79] Hegel frequently refers to the Absolute Spirit or God. Spirit is absolute because it is unconditioned (not related to or influenced by anything outside of itself) since it contains all the other categories or concepts that were developed earlier in the dialectical process (see *Chapter 4 — Dialectics*).

If spirit is the true substance of history, the central theme of Hegel's philosophy of history is freedom. As he writes, "it is the idea of freedom in general which we have to consider, and particularly its operation within the medium of the human spirit; in more specific terms, it is the Idea of human freedom".[80] However, it is not enough for someone to be free they must also be aware of their freedom, they must also have the idea of their freedom. For Hegel:

everything depends on the spirit's self-awareness; if the spirit knows that it is free, it is altogether different from what it would be without this knowledge. For if it does not know that it is free, it is in the position of a slave who is content with his slavery and does not know that his condition is an improper one. It is the sensation of freedom alone which makes the spirit free...[81]

Further, for Hegel "World history is the progress of the consciousness of freedom".[82] There is progress because at different times the trend was towards increasing

degrees of knowledge of freedom — firstly, that of the Orientals, who knew only that One is free, then that of the Greek and Roman world, which knew that Some are free, and finally, our own knowledge that All men as such are free, and that man is by nature free...[83]

To be clear, for Hegel the 'one' of the Oriental world is the emperor and the 'some' of the Greek and Roman world are the freemen, not the slaves who they depended upon for the manner of their existence. Hegel holds it is what he calls the 'Germanic nations' that first realised that all men are free. (However, we would argue, following Marx and Engels, that this is only a formal political freedom and that economic exploitation means that the vast majority of people are still very much not free.) In short, spirit is the substance of history and Hegel's chief concern is the degree of freedom it has. The latter is judged, in part, by our own self-awareness of freedom. Further, history is the progress of this self-awareness.

It is important to grasp that at the heart of Hegel's philosophy of history is a triple identity of the Idea, Reason and God. To see this consider that Hegel holds that the Idea is "the proper philosophical meaning of 'reason'".[84] He also argues that "God and the nature of the divine will are one and the same thing; it is what we call in philosophy the Idea".[85] Joseph McCarney argues that with this identity "one reaches rock bottom, the deepest layer of thought, in the intellectual scheme of the *Introduction*".[86] Having reached rock bottom, to use McCarney's phrase, we can now move on to consider the other elements of Hegel's philosophy of history.

Above we mentioned that for Hegel spirit is the true substance of history. But how is Hegel conceiving of spirit here? And how is it connected to Hegel's notion of God? Hegel writes "that spiritual principle which we call God is none other than the truly substantial, inherently and essentially individual and subjective truth. It is the source of all thought, and its thought is inherently creative; we encounter it as such in world history".[87] If God is the source of all thought and we encounter it in world history, what place is there for human agency? That is, if God makes history, what is it that humans do? It might be all too easy here to dismiss Hegel as being of little worth to those who like Marx wanted to change the world, but this would be a rash mistake, or so we will argue.[88]

The argument turns on different notions of the nature of God, a 'transcendent' one and an 'immanent' one. The notion of a transcendent god is one that is in some sense an individual or person who is distinct from and superior to the world it has created. Further, it is autonomous from the world, that is in no way dependent upon it. Such a reading would be in keeping with much religious thought about the nature of God but not with Hegel's.

According to the immanent notion of God, God is in some sense constituted by nature and the human world and has no reality apart from them. Those familiar with these ideas might note that such an immanent reading appears to tend towards pantheism, first formulated by the seventeenth-century Dutch philosopher Baruch Spinoza. The central idea of pantheism is the belief that God should be identified with the universe, conceived not as an aggregate of particular things but as a unified if impersonal whole. According to an immanent notion of God, although God creates history, since it is constituted by nature and society, humans also create it, at least in part, since they form society.

The upshot here is that human agency can still be an important part of how history is created. It must be acknowledged that this is merely the barest outline of an argument and it is not a universally accepted account. However, we feel it is the reading that makes most sense of both Hegel's belief in God and his belief that humans are active agents in the world.

A final remark to be made here is that there may be in part a pragmatic explanation for the ambiguity in Hegel's exposition on the subject of God. Although seemingly ensconced in the Prussian establishment at the end of his life, he was nonetheless vulnerable to the charge of pantheism. This mattered. In nineteenth-century Prussia such a charge of religious unorthodoxy would have been virtually indistinguishable from atheism to the powerful evangelical faction in the Prussian court. Given this it might be clear why Hegel declared that "Christianity is the religion which has revealed the nature and being of God to man".[89]

Historicism and Idealism

One of the things that we attempted to do in *Chapter 1 — A Biography of Contradiction* was to place Hegel within his times. This placing within an historical context is itself one of the most important lessons that Marx learnt from Hegel.

As McCarney notes, Hegel is "beyond all comparison, the historical philosopher, the one for whom history figures most ambitiously and elaborately as a philosophical category".[90] Perhaps the most striking and characteristic feature of his thought is that it seeks to explain its purpose, principles and problems in historical terms. Rather than seeing philosophy as about things that always have and always will exist, Hegel thinks of it as the expression of a specific historical period or culture. This is what has become known as 'historicism'. And as Beiser rightly states: "Hegel's historicism amounted to nothing less than a revolution in the history of philosophy".[91]

Hegel thought that history conforms to laws of development. For him reason is central, writing that "reason governs the world, and that world history is therefore a rational process," and that history is "the rational and necessary evolution of the world spirit".[92] Hegel's prose can be difficult to understand; however, he is able at least on occasion to combine clarity with a powerful turn of phrase. For instance, he writes: "Just like Mercury, the guide for departed souls, the Idea is truly the leader of nations and of the world; and it is the spirit, with its rational and necessary will, which has directed and continues to direct the events of world history".[93]

That history conforms to laws of development was a key insight for Marx and Engels (although their 'laws' were quite different from Hegel's). To see this consider the following from *Preface to a Contribution to the Critique of Political Economy*:

> In the social production of their life, men enter into definite relations that are indispensable and independent of their will, relations of production which correspond to a definite stage of the development of their material productive forces. The sum total of these relations of production constitutes the economic structure of society, the real foundation, on which rises a legal and political superstructure and to which correspond definite forms of social consciousness. The mode of production of material life conditions the social, political and intellectual life process in general. It is not the consciousness of men that determines their being, but, on the contrary, their social being that determines their consciousness. At a certain stage of development, the material productive forces of society come into conflict with the existing relations of production or — what is but a legal expression for the same thing — with the property relations within which they have been at work hitherto. From forms of development of the productive forces these relations turn into their fetters. Then begins an epoch of social revolution![94]

Not only did Hegel hold that history conformed to laws of

development but he also thought that there was progress in history. A progress that divided world history into different stages, or to use his terminology, 'epochs' which we noted above were the Oriental, Greek and Roman, and Germanic worlds.

Similarly Marx divided history into what he called modes of production, that is, the specific manner in which the materials for human society are created and how these shape a political and ideological superstructure.

Whilst for Hegel there were three epochs, for Marx there were five modes of production: Primitive Communism, Slavery, Feudalism, Capitalism and Communism.[95] With Communism being that mode of production under which "the free development of each is the condition for the free development of all",[96] and when society will be organised on the basis of "From each according to his ability, to each according to his needs!"[97]

Hegel is often labelled or, perhaps in the sense we are about to explain, accused of being an idealist. An idealist in the sense that "everything existed as ideas".[98] However, this is not only far too simplistic, it seems to us to be straightforwardly wrong.

To see this consider, as noted above, that Marx and Engels do not deny the importance of ideas in shaping the world, but for them material reality provides the basis upon which a superstructure of ideas develops, which in turn can play a role in shaping material reality.. Similarly, Hegel does not deny the importance of the material world but holds, wrongly we would argue, that it is ideas that ultimately are the most important factor in shaping history.[99]

So we want to argue that Hegel is *not* an idealist in the sense of holding that everything existed as ideas. However, we do think that he is an idealist in a weaker sense. And this sense is that whilst he readily accepts that the physical or material world exists — the world of tables, trees and i-Phones — for Hegel the driving force of history is not the material world but rather ideas and, in particular, reason.

This way of putting things seems to fit exactly with Marx's famous phrasing in *Capital* of Hegel being placed on his feet. In the Postface to the Second Edition Marx writes:

> For Hegel, the process of thinking, which he even trans-
> forms into an independent subject under the name
> of 'the Idea', is the creator of the real world, and the
> real world is only the external appearance of the idea.
> With me the reverse is true: the ideal is nothing but
> the material world reflected in the mind of man, and
> translated into forms of thought.[100]

Given this, Marx argues that "With him it is standing on
its head. It must be turned right side up again, if you would
discover the rational kernel within the mystical shell".[101]
Having said all this Hegel remains the most curious idealist for
in the *Introduction* not only does he talk about social class but
he also acknowledges that the very climate of the earth affects
the development of freedom.[102]

The Dialectic — Driving History Forward

In *Chapter 4 — Dialectics* we will consider Hegel's dialectic in
detail but it is necessary here to give a brief outline because of
the role it plays in his understanding of historical change. Hegel
holds the dialectic to be the method by which we expound our
fundamental categories.

Further, that it is a method in which every category is shown
to be self-contradictory and in turn it develops into the next,
where the resultant category is not only a new concept but one
which is in some sense higher and richer than its predecessors.
Further, and importantly for our present purposes, Hegel holds,
mistakenly we will argue, that this development is necessary.

In his philosophy of history the dialectic plays a similar role.
It is the dialectic which drives history forward, it is what drives
the progress of the self-awareness of freedom both within
and across epochs. It is important to note that this driving
forward of history is the result of internal contradictions that
move history forward in a progressive manner. Moreover, this

progress is for Hegel necessary.

Master and Slave[103]

The master and slave dialectic has come to be seen by many as one of the most important features of Hegel's philosophy of history. At its heart the master and slave dialectic involves what Hegel calls 'recognition' and the desire and struggle for it — where recognition means something like 'the acknowledgement of the existence and worth' of someone. Thus, recognition (*anerkennung* in German) for Hegel involves two things: first, the identification of another person as a person and second, an explicit recognition of their worth as a person.

Hegel argues that people first try to gain recognition from someone else by somehow trying to compel another person or self-consciousness to give it to them. However, since this other self-consciousness is itself driven by the same compulsion, the immediate outcome is a struggle for recognition which, with little by way of argument, Hegel dramatically claims is a "life-and-death struggle".[104] Hegel continues that if such a struggle is entered into, then it destroys the very possibility of recognition. This is because in a life-and-death struggle ultimately one of the combatants will die and if this combatant is dead, then they cannot recognise the other combatant as a self-consciousness with worth. Hegel goes on argue that one of the combatants will realise the futility of the life-and-death struggle and surrender to the other by recognising them as a person and their worth. The person who surrenders becomes the 'slave' and the one who does not becomes the 'master'. Thus, the life-and-death struggle is succeeded by the relationship of master and slave, a situation which Hegel argues allows the emergence of man's life within a society and "a beginning of states"[105] because it implies common wants and a common concern for their satisfaction.

In one sense the prominence of the master and slave dialectic is odd because for much of the time since Hegel conceived it it has received scant attention. However, this changed due, above all else, to the work of Alexandre Kojeve, the most influential commentator on Hegel's philosophy of history since the start of the twentieth century. It should be acknowledged that the master and slave dialectic is plainly an important point for the development of Hegel's system. This is because the desire and struggle for recognition lays the groundwork, as noted above, for historical development through the creation of society and politics. However, it is not at all clear to us that Kojeve is right to claim that the master slave dialectic is the central driving force of history. Kojeve claims that neither master nor slave is able to obtain recognition, which he argues is the most human of desires, and this makes the relationship inherently restless and unstable. History for Kojeve is the product and expression of this struggle. As he states history is "the history of the inter-action between warlike Master and working Slaves".[106]

There are, however, a couple of reasons to reject Kojeve's account. The first is that there is little in what Hegel writes to support the view that the master slave dialectic is inherently unstable. Once Hegel has introduced the notion in the *Phenomenology of Spirit* it scarcely figures in that work apart from a section on 'Conscience'. However, Hegel employs it here in a context of having been achieved, not of an on-going striving. For example, he writes the "self" of a person is said to be "the state of being recognised".[107] Shortly afterwards the common element of distinct self-consciousness, and the substance in which activity has existence and reality, is said to be "the moment of being *recognised* and *acknowledged* by others".[108]

A second reason to reject Kojeve's account is that Hegel states that the life and death struggle for recognition only occurs in that natural state "where human beings exist as single individuals". It is, however, absent in civil society and the state because that recognition is "already present".[109] This would seem to relegate the struggle for recognition to a primitive stage of human development. What it does not suggest is that this struggle is one that occurs at all times in human development and also animates this whole development. Here Hegel makes the power relationship between human beings paramount rather than seeing this relationship as a consequence of man's interaction with nature (as Marx does).

World Historical Figures

Hegel is occasionally criticised for holding something like a 'Great Man' theory of history. Popularised in the nineteenth-century by Scottish writer Thomas Carlyle, it is the idea that history is largely to be explained by the impact of 'great men' or heroes — highly influential individuals who had a decisive historical impact. Hegel did indeed write of heroes or in his particular terminology 'world historical individuals.'

He refers to Alexander the Great, Julius Caesar and, as we have seen in *Chapter 1 — A Biography of Contradiction*, Napoleon Bonaparte as being examples of such world historical individuals who he did see as playing a vital role in history.

Hegel writes that "world-historical individuals are those who have willed and accomplished not just the ends of their imagination or personal opinions, but only those which were appropriate and necessary. Such individuals know what is necessary and timely, and have an inner vision of what it is".[110]

However, for a number of reasons it would be mistaken to hold that Hegel does hold a great men theory of history. First, it will be remembered that for Hegel it is spirit not individuals — world historical or otherwise — that is the true substance of history, with the dialectic driving it.

Further, Hegel does *not* suggest that Caesar or any of the other world historical figures had the kind of insight into the significance of their own historical period that would involve consciousness of the Idea as such. Thus he continues:

> It is possible to distinguish between the insight of such individuals and the realisation that even such manifestations of the spirit as this are no more than moments within the universal Idea. To understand this is the prerogative of philosophy. World-historical individuals have no need to do so, as they are men of practice.[111]

A second reason to reject the claim that Hegel held a great men theory of history is that Hegel is only too aware of the role that a person's individual circumstances, as well as their wider political and cultural context, play in shaping who they are and what they are able to do.

Thus, he writes "Each individual is the son of his own nation at a specific stage in this nation's development. No one can escape from the spirit of his nation, any more than he can escape from the earth itself".[112] However, at the same time he insists that world historical figures:

> do, however, know and will their own enterprise, because the time is ripe for it, and it is already inwardly present. Their business is to know this universal principle, which is the necessary and culminating stage in the development of their world, to make it their end, and to devote their energy to its realisation.[113]

These two quotes show that Hegel is both trying to acknowledge the role that history plays in shaping who we are and insisting on human agency — that it is humans that make history.

At the same time he holds that there is a direction to history steered by the Idea. Marx and Engels were also involved in a similar although importantly different enterprise. For Marx wrote in *The Eighteenth Brumaire of Louis Bonaparte*:

> Men make their own history, but they do not make it as they please; they do not make it under self-selected circumstances, but under circumstances existing already, given and transmitted from the past. The tradition of all dead generations weighs like a nightmare on the brains of the living.[114]

It is no sheer coincidence that Marx wrote this and we would argue that it is one of the most important things that

Marx and Engels learnt from Hegel in the whole of their thought, not just in the philosophy of history.

The Cunning of Reason

Our discussion of world historical individuals may have prompted the reader to wonder how it could be that such individuals, with their limited understanding, manage to advance the cause of the Idea. Further, this is a problem that arises for those who are not judged world historical individuals as well and, we would argue, for all historical actors.

Hegel's answer is what he calls the 'cunning of reason'. He introduces it in the following passage:

> The particular has its own interests in world history; it is of a finite nature, and as such, it must perish. Particular interests contend with one another, and some are destroyed in the process. But it is from this very conflict and destruction of particular things that the universal emerges, and it remains unscathed itself. For it is not the universal Idea which enters into opposition, conflict, and danger; it keeps itself in the background, untouched and unharmed, and sends forth the particular interest of passion to fight and wear themselves out in its stead. It is what we may call the *cunning of reason* that it sets the passions to work in its service, so that the agents by which it gives itself existences must pay the penalty and suffer the loss.[115]

Here the cunning of reason is presented as the basic answer to how, through the actions of particular historical actors, the Idea comes to be realised.

As is suggested by the above quote a key aspect of the cunning of reason is that it operates "behind the back"[116] of the consciousness of the particular participants. (It thus has something in common with Adam Smith's 'invisible hand' in the economic field which was said to act in the same way.) As such it brings centre stage the question of teleology, namely, the study of the ends or purpose of things. To believe in a *telos* is to hold that history has a direction of travel. And if one holds that there is such a direction, then one must hold that something like the cunning of reason is a part of your philosophy of history.[117] There must be something pulling the strings behind the scenes so to speak.

A perfectly understandable reaction to talk of telos is that this is reminiscent of some sort of mystical mumbo jumbo. Further, that for all his other insights Hegel will be of little use to those trying to understand the world at the start of the twentieth-first century. However, this would be a far too hasty and ultimately misguided assertion. To see this consider two examples from biology which seem quite rightly to support the idea of telos. The first is provided by Hegel himself when he writes that "just as the seed bears within it the whole nature of the tree and the taste and form of its fruit, so also do the first glimmerings of spirit contain virtually the whole of history".[118] Here the organism is itself important for Hegel because its very existence shows that the ends of something can be internally as opposed to externally related to its means. That is, it is internally or self organised. This example suggests the possibility that human history may also be understood as a self-organising or self-determining whole that somehow derives its telos from within itself.

The second example is the theory of evolution by means of natural selection. Natural selection provides an account of how particular traits became adapted to their environment. Consequently, it permits assertions about the purpose an adaption serves, without any commitment to the idea of a designer.

The State and the End of History

For Hegel it is not the individual or classes that history is concerned with but rather the state. As he himself writes "In world history, however, the individuals we are concerned with are nations, totalities, states".[119] The significance of the state for Hegel is that the state is "the realisation of freedom".[120] It has this status because Hegel holds that rights have to be realised as part of a structure of rights as well as constitutional order that can only be provided by a state. This is perhaps all the more understandable given that during his lifetime both the United States constitution and France's Declaration of the Rights of Man and of the Citizen were formulated, and they represented a major advance on feudal traditions.

For Hegel a state is constituted by a people which have achieved a certain level of organisation and unity. He acknowledges that peoples may have existed for some time and may even have achieved significant developments in certain directions. We should make it clear in his history of the world Hegel does not insist on any one-to-one correspondence between people and state. This is no less true of Hegel's mature theory of the state as presented in the *Philosophy of Right*. He writes "*A human being counts as such because he is a human being*, not because he is a Jew, Catholic, Protestant, German, Italian, etc".[121] It should be noted that in taking this view, Hegel was setting himself directly against anti-Semitism — the most powerful form of racism of his time.

The reader of the *Introduction* is likely to be struck by the state's role in determining the scope of world history; that is, delimiting when humanity's past starts to become truly historical (and when it ends). The simple answer is that history proper begins for Hegel when the state becomes a historical actor. However, it is a common criticism of Hegel's philosophy of history that it gives too large an importance to the state. In response it should be remembered that for Hegel history is the progress of the consciousness of freedom, a progress that is necessary. This internal necessity is what we have seen him refer to as dialectical movement. It is our suggestion that the central philosophical significance of the state is to be derived from its role in ensuring that history should be conceived as an internally, necessary, dialectical progression. The key step in the argument here is the role that memory plays in Hegel's dialectic. In the *Phenomenology of Spirit* Hegel argues that the task of memory is to preserve the spiritual achievement of each individual phase of dialectal reasoning. Thus, each phase of dialectical reasoning can start at the next conceptual level and the whole dialectical process can constitute an internally connected sequence of steps that are a progression of consciousness. In the individual human, memory serves this function and it may be readily thought of as residing in, as well as partly constitutive of, the self. As McCarney argues:

> For a historical dialectic to be intelligible, some collective analogue of the individual self as the bearer of memory has to be found. Here must be some institutional locus of memory that is itself an individual self-moving entity persisting through significant stretches of historical time. [T]he state is the only possible candidate, the only sufficiently close relative of the self of memory in the social world.[122]

One might be unconvinced by the central role of the state and be tempted as some sympathetic critics have done, for example R. G. Collingwood,[123] to reject this role with everything else remaining. However, this will not do as the structure falls or stands as a theoretical whole. It should be pointed out here that for Hegel, therefore, the state is not a force confronting people as an external power (as 'armed bodies of men' for Marx and Engels), but as an embodiment and vehicle for the spirit.

If the beginning of history seems like an academic discussion *par excellence*, then the end of history is, or was at least for a time, a highly charged political question. The collapse of the Soviet Union in 1989 and the subsequent disintegration of the Warsaw Pact was greeted by some as the death of socialism and the victory of free-market capitalism. We would argue that it was nothing of the sort. Rather the collapse of the Soviet Union should be seen as having created the political opportunity for the revival of socialism from below marked by working-class self-activity. Other commentators, most notably Francis

Fukuyama in *The End of History and the Last Man* (1992), argued that it showed that Hegel and Marx's view of history as a "single, coherent, evolutionary process, when taking into account the experience of all peoples in all times"[124] had been shown to be mistaken. It should be clear that it was Fukuyama who was mistaken; for the 25 years since he made the claim we have seen frequent although ultimately unsuccessful revolutions, from the Kurdish uprisings in 1991 to the Arab Spring, as well as the longest slump in capitalist history.

In *The Philosophy of History* it seems that for Hegel history does have an end. Consider the following quotations to see this:

> The History of the World travels from East to West, for Europe is absolutely the end of History, Asia the beginning.
>
> For the Christian world is the world of completion; the grand principle of being realized, consequently the end of days is fully come.
>
> This formally absolute principle brings us to *the last state in History, our world, our own time.*[125]

Further, if these quotations are viewed in light of Hegel's account of the development of the consciousness of freedom: "The East knew and to the present day knows only that *One* is Free; the Greek and Roman world, that *some* are free; the German World knows that *All* are free",[126] the conclusion appears clear. Namely, that Hegel holds that there is a point beyond which there can be no further progress, no further development in the awareness of freedom. This point is the German World when, according to Hegel, 'all are free'. Given this one might be tempted to agree with Frederick Nietzsche[127] when he wonders why if the Germanic world in which Hegel lived was the end point of history, is not all that follows Hegel's own existence something akin to 'post-history'. However, we would argue that this would be mistaken. If Hegel had been alive to respond to Nietzsche, it would seem perfectly coherent for him to have replied that the Germanic world is the terminus for world history without having to claim that history will have stopped during his lifetime. This is because although Hegel was living in the final epoch of world history, he was not living at the end of the epoch. That is, there may still be historical actions and events of great significance still to take place.

Eurocentrism

There is currently a welcome call to 'decolonise' universities. It is about challenging the conservative, elitist and implicitly racist view that constitutes the background against which much of academic research takes place. It rejects a common-sense establishment view that all positive developments in history have come from white Europeans. But for some in this movement it is also necessary to reject the thought of all nineteenth-century white men, including those like Hegel and Marx, who argued for the liberation of all of humanity.[128]

It will be recalled that for Hegel history is the increasing consciousness of freedom. In the Oriental world only the emperor is free because only he is aware of his freedom, in the Greek and Roman world it is only the freemen who are free but it is in the Germanic nations that it was first realised all are free. It seems clear here that Hegel's account is centred on Europe, with Europe playing a privileged role. This is especially the case if it is pointed out that in the rest of the world (with the exception of the emperor of the Oriental world), none feature in history because none are aware of their freedom. Further, Hegel seems to suggest that the world's other peoples can only acquire freedom if Europeans first impose their civilisation on them. For example, he writes, for "the Negroes are far more receptive to European culture than the Indians...[and] it will still be a long time before the Europeans succeed in producing any genuine feeling of self" in indigenous Americans.[129] Here it seems that Hegel is clearly supporting colonialism as part of the process of realising freedom. This should be contrasted with Hegel's clams that the human capacity for self-determination is universal. So, what are we to make of this situation?

It is our contention that it is possible to separate the core of Hegel's account of freedom from his inaccurate and prejudiced views which dismissed non-Europeans as being incapable of coming to freedom by themselves.[130] His dismissive attitude does not undermine his core points that freedom develops historically in tandem with the consciousness of it, as embodied in different cultures and social institutions. Further, when we separate these core points from his prejudiced account of actual historical situations then this core can serve a progressive non-Eurocentric purpose.[131]

What did Marx Learn from Hegel?

In conclusion we have argued that Marx (and Engels) learnt a number of important things from Hegel regarding the philosophy of history. First is that philosophy and all attempts to understand the world must be placed within an historical context. Second, history conforms to laws or patterns of development and that these laws embody progress. For Hegel this progress is in terms of the consciousness of freedom, for Marx and Engels it is the material forces and relations of production. Third, ideas as well as material reality are important in shaping history. However, whereas Hegel held that ideas are ultimately the most important factor Marx argued that Hegel was standing on his head and that it is in fact material reality which is the most important factor. Fourth, that what drives history are internal contradictions, in other words a dialectic. Marx and Engels differed from Hegel, however, by insisting that this movement was not necessary. Fifth, those who are engaged in understanding history but at the same time are trying to shape the present must both acknowledge the role that history plays in shaping who we are and insist on human agency.

Chapter 4
Dialectics

'Dialectics' is a term used to describe a method of argument that involves, in some way, a contradictory process between opposing sides. One source of inspiration for Hegel's dialectics was the ancient Greek philosopher Plato, in particular his dialogue *Parmenides*.[132] In *Parmenides* Plato takes an interlocutor through a series of dilemmas, arguing that neither of two contradictory statements can rightly be called correct or truthful. He claims to show that nothing can have parts or be whole; nothing is at rest nor in motion; nothing can be the same as another or even itself, nor can be different from itself or another; and, nothing is in time or in space.

Such arguments are echoed by Kant in his most important work, the *Critique of Pure Reason*.[133] Kant called these paradoxes 'antinomies' of (pure) reason or the conflict of laws of (pure) reason and argued that there were just four such conflicts.[134] Consider his first antinomy. Kant argues that if we start from the premise "The world has a beginning in time and is also enclosed within bounds as regards space,"[135] that is, if the world can be shown to be finite, then it can be shown that the world is in fact infinite. Likewise, if we start from the premise

"The world has no beginning and no bounds in space, but is infinite as regards both time and space,"[136] it can be shown that the world is in fact finite. In both Plato's *Parmenides* and Kant's *Critique of Pure Reason*, the examination of a single proposition leads to a conclusion that actually affirms the very opposite, yet starting with the opposite confirms the proposition that we began with. In both the ancient world and during the Enlightenment, such reasoning is used to promote scepticism — the theory that we can know nothing of the world around us. However, as we shall see, Hegel has a very different use in mind for it, namely as a method of expounding our fundamental categories, that is, humanity's common store of thoughts that have been transmitted from generation to generation.[137]

Three Sides of the Dialectic

In *Chapter 1 — A Biography of Contradiction* we noted that Hegel lived and worked at a time of tremendous change. Many of the old certainties had been shattered by the overthrow of much of the feudal hierarchy. In politics — with the French Revolution playing a central role — freedom had been made into a principle of legitimate authority and activity; in art there was now an unprecedented freedom of style and subject-matter; and in philosophy, free self-determining and self-critical reason had been established as the highest authority in human life. What Hegel learns from his philosophical predecessors, particularly Rene Descartes and Kant, is twofold. First, reason can help free us from arbitrary authority by subjecting it to scrutiny. Second, reason itself must be subject to the same searing scrutiny. A consequence of this second point for Hegel is that a new account of thought must be developed, one that makes no assumptions or presuppositions; that is a new science of logic. Hegel insists that we should follow Descartes and suspend judgment about what we have previously taken for granted until some way has been found to show whether or not our traditional ways of thinking are justified. He insists that "science should be preceded by universal doubt, i.e., by total presuppositionlessness".[138]

But how is Hegel's logic to proceed if it is to take nothing for granted? Hegel's method is the dialectic which, as he states in the Preface to the first edition of the *Science of Logic*, is his "absolute method of knowing".[139] Further, it is a method of exposition in which each category in turn is shown to be implicitly self-contradictory and to develop necessarily into the next.

To form a more precise picture of the intended structure of the dialectic consider the following general account from *The Encyclopaedia Logic*: "With regard to its form, the logical has three sides: (α) the side of abstraction or of the understanding, (β) the dialectical or negatively rational side, [and] (γ) the speculative or positively rational one".[140] It is no straightforward matter to get clear on what Hegel means by this description, but here is our attempt.

The 'understanding'[141] is one-sided in the sense that it separates objects from one another or, put another way, it views them in isolation. This is of course important because how can we proceed in theorising about something if we are not clear about precisely the thing that we are to be concerned with. Referring to the great German poet Goethe, Hegel writes approvingly "someone who wants to do great things must know how to restrict himself. In contrast, someone who wants to do everything really wants to do nothing, and brings off nothing".[142]

The key aspect of the dialectical or negatively rational side is that the isolated views of the first part of the dialectic — the 'understanding' — pass "into their opposites",[143] into their negation. The first two sides of the dialectics, as Burbidge writes, "are reciprocally interconnected in a conceptual synthesis where each constitutes and requires the other".[144] Moreover this passing is the result of the internal make-up of the 'understanding' itself, not due to some external factor. The dialectic as Hegel writes "is the *immanent* transcending, in which the one-sidedness and restrictedness of the determinations of the understanding displays itself as what it is, i.e., as their negation".[145] In the dialectical moment the contradictory nature of what Hegel is considering comes to light:

Thus we say, for instance, that man is mortal; and we regard dying as having its ground only in external circumstances. In this way of looking at things, a man has two specific properties, namely, he is alive and *also* mortal. But the proper interpretation is that life as such bears the germ of death within itself, and that the finite sublates itself because it contradicts itself inwardly.[146]

The verb 'sublate', meaning assimilate a smaller entity into a larger one, is used as the translation of Hegel's technical use of the German verb '*aufheben*' which is a crucial concept in his dialectical method.[2] Hegel holds that *aufheben* has a double meaning: "on the one hand it means to preserve, to maintain, and equally it also means to cause to cease, to put an end to".[147] In short, the dialectical moment is the passing from the one-sidedness of the 'understanding' to its opposite and that this passing is the result of something internal and also contradictory. It is important to stress that this passing is the result of something internal to the method because it is one of the features of Hegel's account of dialectics that he takes to make it an improvement on, for example, Plato's.

An additional point we would like to make here is that sometimes those discussing the dialectic claim that what it in fact amounts to is a seesawing or a back and forth between arguments. This is not a new phenomenon, as Hegel himself makes the same observation. However, this is definitely *not* how Hegel saw the dialectic. Commenting on Kant's antinomies he states that they "in no way involve a simple seesawing between [opposite] grounds".[148]

The third and final side of dialectic is the speculative or positively rational. Hegel writes that this third side "apprehends the unity of the determinations in their position, the affirmative that is contained in their dissolution and in their transition".[149] This third side is a coming together of the 'understanding' and

2 We have placed the word understanding in inverted commas to show that we are referring to Hegel's technical meaning rather than the everyday sense.

its opposite — the dialectical moment; but this coming together is in fact also the dissolution of the contradiction (sometimes referred to as 'the negation of the negation').

As noted above Hegel holds that the dialectic is essentially a method of expounding humanity's fundamental categories. As we have argued above it is a method of exposition in which every category is shown to be self-contradictory and in turn it develops into the next. The result of the dialectical process "is a fresh Notion but higher and richer than its predecessor; for it is richer by the negation or opposite of the latter, therefore contains it, but also something more, and is the unity of itself and its opposite".[150] Hegel holds that this development is necessary. The nature of the categories or concepts forces them to pass into their opposite. This necessity is an important point to note since it leads Hegel to regard his dialectics as a kind of logic, for necessity — that is, where one thing has to follow on from another — is widely seen as the hallmark of logic in Western philosophy. These categories form a hierarchical series with each new one more comprehensive or universal than the last, culminating in the all-embracing category of the Absolute Idea. It is absolute in the same sense as the Absolute Spirit (or God) is: there is nothing outside it to which it could possibly be relative.

As we have acknowledged, it is no easy matter to clearly present what Hegel meant by his dialectic but it is worth noting that our own ordinary thinking has some similarity with dialectics. Hegel writes:

> we find the consciousness of dialectic in those universally familiar proverbs: 'Pride goes before a fall', 'Too much wit outwits itself', etc. — Feeling, too…has its dialectic. It is well known how the extremes of pain and joy pass into one another; the heart filled with joy relieves itself in tears, and the deepest melancholy tends in certain circumstances to make itself known by a smile.[151]

It is also worth noting as we did in the *Preface* that Marx explicitly acknowledges that he learnt a great deal about dialectics from Hegel. In *Capital* Marx comments that as he was writing this, the greatest of his of works, he "openly avowed myself the pupil of that mighty thinker".[152] Marx goes on to assert that Hegel was "the first to present [the dialectic's] general forms of motion in a comprehensive and conscious manner".[153]

An Example: Being, Nothingness and Becoming

It will we hope prove helpful to illustrate the general model of the logic of Hegel's dialectic by means of an example from the start of the *Science of Logic*. As noted above, Hegel wanted to accept only what reason itself could determine to be true without assuming anything. He held that the most basic thought that anyone could think was that something existed, that it be. But he did not want to assume it had any specific properties. He did not want to think, for example, that it was red or heavy or was in London.

But as soon as we try just to think of being, pure being, it seems that we slide into nothingness. Being turns into nothingness because this thing that we are thinking of has no properties. It is not red or any other colour. It is not heavy, or light or any other weight. And it is not in London or New York or anywhere else. So being seems to become nothing.

Next Hegel asks us to think about nothing, nothing at all. Thinking of nothing is not the same as *not* thinking. We are still thinking even if we are not thinking about being red or heavy or being in London. When thinking of absolutely nothing it still seems that we are thinking about existence, about being. So, when we think of nothing this seems to slide into thinking about being, about thoughts that exist.

It appears that thinking of being seems to slide into nothingness and thinking of nothing seems to slide into thinking about being. How do we get out of this impasse? Hegel argues that we need to pay close attention to what happens as these thoughts are being thought. If we do, we will notice that our thought of being becomes nothing and our thought of nothing becomes being. Out of being and nothingness we have becoming.

Two Misconceptions

One complication in trying to understand Hegel's dialectic is that, as Stephen Houlgate argues, *The Science of Logic* is "one of the most difficult and daunting [works] in the whole history of philosophy...and the book as a whole continues to present a formidable challenge to even its most sympathetic and assiduous of readers".[154] Given this it is perhaps unsurprising that no aspect of Hegel's philosophy has been more misunderstood and more controversial than the dialectic. So having outlined what we take to be the correct account of Hegel's dialectical method it will be necessary to try to correct two misunderstandings and consider one supposedly fatal flaw.

The first misconception is that Hegel rejected traditional logic. More specifically he rejected the so-called laws of identity and non-contradiction. Something like this claim is made, for example, by George Novack.[155] It is important here is to be clear about what is meant by these terms. The so-called law of identity states that everything is what it is and nothing else. Sunday is Sunday and nothing else. The law of non-contradiction states that it is not the case that something holds and that something doesn't hold. It's not the case that it's both Sunday and not Sunday.

To be clear, Hegel did criticise Aristotelian or syllogistic logic[3][156] and there are indeed even passages in which Hegel seems to think about rejecting the law of non-contradiction. Yet despite this lack of clarity we want to argue that not only is his dialectic not committed to rejecting the laws of identity and of non-contradiction, but that in fact it actually presupposes them. However, before we do so, consider what Hegel writes of the laws of identity and non-contradiction and their status

3 Syllogistic logic allows inferences of one conclusion from two premises. Each premise has one term in common with the conclusion, and one term in common with the other premises.

as *"universal laws of thought"*.[157] Key here is to appreciate that Hegel is concerned with how accurately these so-called laws of thought capture how well people do in fact think.

> If someone says that this proposition cannot be proven, but that *every* consciousness proceeds in accordance with it and, as experience shows agrees with it at once, as soon as it takes it in, then against this alleged experience of the Schools we have to set the universal experience that no consciousness thinks, has notions, or speaks, according to this law, and no existence of any kind at all exists in accordance with it. Speaking in accordance with this supposed law of truth (a planet is — a planet, magnetism is — magnetism, the spirit is — a spirit) is rightly regarded as silly; that is indeed a universal experience. The Schoolroom, which is the only place where these laws are valid, along with its logic which propounds them in earnest, has long since lost all credit with sound common sense as well as with reason.[158]

Note here is that Hegel does not say that the laws of identity and non-contradiction are not true. He dismisses them as only valid in the 'Schoolroom', which we take to refer to academia. These rules are silly because whilst true they tell us nothing about the world. Just as importantly Hegel makes the point that they do not at all capture the way in which people actually think. However, what he is concerned with most is thinking about thinking, as a way to come to know the Absolute Idea. For the laws of identity and of non-contradiction tell us very little and need to be augmented by dialectical thinking, which is able to tell us something more by virtue of its ability to resolve the contradictions we encounter. So although Hegel did not reject traditional logic, for him it could only be a starting point from which to develop a dialectical way of thinking.[159]

We also want to argue that Hegel's philosophy actually presupposes the validity of the law of non-contradiction. This is because one of the central planks of his thought, and in particular his dialectical method, is to remove contradictions. If Hegel really wanted to reject the law of non-contradiction, it would make little sense for him to put the removal of contradictions as a key component of his philosophy!

A second misconception is that Hegel held that his account of dialectics could be captured by the phrase 'thesis-antithesis-synthesis'. As noted above, Hegel's dialectics was in part inspired by Kant's work on paradoxes or antinomies. However, Hegel never used Kant's method of exposition, namely: 'thesis-antithesis'. To be clear, we are not saying that Hegel never uses the words 'thesis' and 'antithesis'. Rather, he doesn't do so jointly with 'synthesis' and so does not try to explain his dialectical method by this means. Someone who does, however, is the notable critic of Marxism, Karl Popper, who famously argued that Marxism was 'pseudo-scientific'. According to Popper the dialectic "is a theory which maintains that something — more especially, human thought — develops in a way characterized by what is called the dialectic triad: thesis, antithesis, and synthesis".[160]

Hegel in *The Encyclopaedia Logic* does state that there are three stages of the dialectic, but as we have seen these are not: 'thesis-antithesis-synthesis'. The key reason to avoid using the formulation 'thesis-antithesis-synthesis' concerns the last of these phrases: synthesis. A synthesis is a combination of components. However, this is *not* the outcome of an Hegelian dialectic. The outcome is not simply a combination of what has gone before. For Hegel, and also for Marx, the dialectic produces something that is new in some strong sense and, as we saw in *Chapter 3 — The Philosophy of History*, it is this that accounts for the direction of history. And this newness is something that is not captured by the word 'synthesis'.

Fatal Flaw? The Contradictory Nature of the Dialectic

Although we have argued that Hegel did not reject Aristotelian or syllogistic logic we want to suggest that not only did he see contradictions everywhere — "everything is inherently contradictory"[161] — but that this is not actually a problem for his philosophy but in fact provides one of its central insights.

We will consider two of the most common strategies for defending Hegel against the claim that he affirms contradictions. The first is that despite his talk about contradictions he means something much more innocuous and superficial. If Hegel does not mean contradictions when he uses the word 'contradictions' but something more innocuous, then why throughout his writings are there so many specific examples of them? Why, as we have seen, in *The Encyclopaedia Logic* does he place his dialectic in the tradition of perhaps the two most notable works of philosophy that deal explicitly with contradictions: Plato's *Parmenides* and Kant's *Critique of Pure Reason*?

The second common way in which to defend Hegel is to claim that he holds that the contradictions in something only occur at different times or are different aspects of the same thing. For example, Beiser writes that the contradictory claims that seem true of the same thing are really "only true of *different* parts or aspects of the same thing".[162] However, Hegel, at least at times, pointedly rejects the suggestion. "Something moves, not because at one moment it is here and at another there, but because at one and the same moment it is here and not here".[163]

So, how are we to understand what Hegel writes of contradictions? It is our contention that Hegel does not locate contradictions so much in reality as in thought, and moreover that they are all-pervasive and necessary. Put another way, contradictions in reality are not to be accepted but contradictions in how people think are real.

One problem for our analysis is that it has been argued that Hegel himself would actually reject such an account. Michael Forster makes this point by arguing that Hegel criticises Kant for "locating the contradictions of the Antinomies in thought rather than the world".[164] However, we think that Forster is too quick here. It is indeed the case that Hegel's point here is to *ultimately* reject Kant's distinction between thought and world, as we explored in *Chapter 2 — Alienation*. However, the important point to note is that Hegel's rejection of the distinction between thought and world is one that is taken only from the standpoint of the Absolute Idea, when an all-embracing view has been achieved. From the perspective of the Absolute Idea, all contradictions are resolved. Or, to put it another way, the separation of thought and being can only be rejected from the viewpoint of totality: as already noted, "The True is the whole".[165] However, these contradictions can only be resolved after they have been the driving force of our journey to understanding the world. As Hegel continues: "But the whole is nothing other than the essence consummating itself through its development".[166, 167]

Two Problems: Triads and Necessity

We have argued that the contradictions inherent to Hegel's dialectic are not some fatal flaw but rather they help provide it with many of its central insights. Nonetheless we do feel that it has rightly been subject to a number of criticisms which ultimately undermine both its supposed necessity and the extent of its applicability. To be clear, however, whilst these criticisms undermine Hegel's dialectic method, they do not invalidate all dialectical methods; in particular, they do not undermine Marx's method which, as we shall argue below, is importantly different from Hegel's.

First, let us consider the triadic structure of Hegel's dialectic, that is, the 'understanding', the dialectical or negatively rational side and the speculative or positively rational one (the negation of the negation). The problem here is not that there is anything wrong in principle with this three-part structure, rather it is that Hegel does not use it consistently and often it is absent. As Julie Maybee notes, there are "places where this general pattern might describe *some* of the transitions from stage to stage, but there are *many more* places where the development does not seem to fit this pattern very well".[168] Further, other sections of Hegel's philosophy do not match the triadic, textbook example at all. As W. T. Stace warns "There are even cases of 'triads' that contain four terms!"[169]

There are other times in the *Science of Logic* Stace argues, such as the section of cognition, when "There is no third term. Hegel here abandons the triadic method. Nor is any explanation of his having done so forthcoming".[170] Yet, as Stace argues, these irregularities do not mean that the dialectic method is wrong, rather, merely that Hegel has not been able to carry out his own method consistently. Our own conclusion is that this inability of Hegel is indicative of the fact that the dialectic and dialectical method is not as widely applicable as he argues. It cannot be used to understand all of thought, rather, it must be used much more selectively and when that is done appropriately it can be uniquely insightful.

Hegel held that the nature of categories we think about forces them to pass into their opposite and onto a new, higher category as a matter of necessity. That is, the result of the contradiction between the 'understanding' and the dialectical or negatively rational side is bound to have a particular outcome — the speculative or positively rational side — at each and every step towards the Absolute Idea, the final category. The second problem we wish to point out lies in the suggestion that the transition to the new category is a *necessary* one. As Robert C. Solomon has forcefully argued, the movement from one category to another "is not in any way a deductive *necessity*". [171]

Some appear to try to get round this by arguing that we should not in fact take Hegel's claim of necessity too strongly (see, for example, Findlay).[172] That is, we should not hold that there is anything predetermined in the route Hegel's thinking takes from his starting point of being, nothingness and becoming (see above) to the Absolute Idea. One difficulty here is that this would clearly go against what Hegel repeatedly stresses. Further, this position seems untenable in terms of Hegel's wider goals for his philosophy. Dispensing with the claim of necessity would, as Michael Forster argues, "wholly undermine the method's ability to demonstrate entire systematicity and thence completeness".[173] In other words, if there is no necessity in Hegel's dialectical method, if there is no guarantee that one category leads to a specific higher category, then there is no guarantee that we will arrive at the Absolute Idea, the all-embracing category that contains all knowledge of the world.

In response, Maybee quite rightly warns that "We should also be careful not to exaggerate the 'necessity' of formal, symbolic logic".[174] This is because even in formal logic there can be more than just one path from a set of premises or starting-point to the same conclusion. To see this, consider the analogy of a car journey from London to Edinburgh. Starting on the A10 in London and heading north the driver is quickly faced with a choice between taking the M1 or the M11. If, for example, the M1 is taken, after a while the driver is faced with another choice of joining the M6 and then the A74(M) or heading to the A1, with both of these routes taking the driver, eventually, to Edinburgh. Although the starting-point and the destination are the same the routes are different. There is nothing 'necessary' about any of these route choices made, but despite this the driver will reach Edinburgh when all the steps are taken together. Similarly, in logic there is often no 'necessity' from one step to the next despite the fact that the conclusion might be entailed by all of the steps being taken together. We do agree with Maybee that a 'strong' sense of necessity is missing from formal logic. However, this does little to help Hegel because, as is clear from what he himself writes, he holds that there is a 'strong' sense of necessity in his dialectical method: change may be large and the clash of contradictions sharp, but it *needs* to go in one direction.

Unintended Consequences — The Marxist Dialectic

In *The German Ideology* Marx and Engels wrote that "society has hitherto always developed within the framework of a contradiction — in antiquity the contradiction between freemen and slaves, in the Middle Ages that between nobility and serfs, in modern times that between the bourgeoisie and the proletariat".[175] As we have just seen, Hegel held that the nature of categories forces them to pass into their opposite and onto a new, higher category as a matter of necessity (though admittedly, it was often a necessity that did not seem to be present). However, there is no such necessity in the dialectic of Marx and Engels. Writing in the *Communist Manifesto* Marx and Engels take up the above theme:

> The history of all hitherto existing society is the history of class struggles.
>
> Freeman and slave, patrician and plebeian, lord and serf, guild-master and journeyman, in a word, oppressor and oppressed, stood in constant opposition to one another, carried on an uninterrupted, now hidden, now open fight, a fight that each time ended, either in *a revolutionary reconstitution of society at large, or in the common ruin of the contending classes.*[176]

Unlike for Hegel, how contradictions were resolved was a contingent matter, that is, it was not predetermined. Rather, their resolution was dependent on other things, in particular how the struggle between classes was fought, won and lost. Putting the point bluntly, if Marx thought there was a historical necessity about the victory of socialism why on earth would he have spent his entire adult life trying to bring about this change?

The contingency of history allowed for, we would argue, one of the two most important differences between the dialectic of Marx and Hegel, that of unintended consequences. The other is that whilst Hegel's dialectic was an idealist one, Marx's was most avowedly a materialist one. This difference pervades all of their thoughts.

Marx's writings are littered with examples whereby an understanding of a situation leads to action but the action results in unintended consequences that undermine or limit the desired outcome. For example, under capitalism it is the capitalists who own and control the means of production. However, they do not own the labour power necessary to put them to work. What they require is another class, namely, the proletariat or working class, a class that has to sell its labour power in order to survive. The emerging capitalist class took actions, such as the enclosures movement in England between the sixteenth and nineteenth centuries, in order to force the peasantry off the land leaving them with little option to begin to sell their labour power to the capitalists. The most important unintended consequence of this was that the capitalists' attempts to bring about a working class to create wealth for them, created a class that would have the power to overthrow them. As Marx and Engels write:

> The essential conditions for the existence and for the sway of the bourgeois class is the formation and augmentation of capital; the condition for capital is wage-labour. Wage-labour rests exclusively on competition between the labourers. The advance of industry, whose *involuntary promoter* is the bourgeoisie, replaces the isolation of the labourers, due to competition, by the revolutionary combination, due to association. The development of Modern Industry, therefore, cuts from under its feet the very foundation on which the bourgeoisie produces and appropriates products. What the *bourgeoisie therefore produces, above all, are its own grave-diggers.*[177]

The pattern of intended action and unintended consequence above is clear. Another example of unintended consequences is the capitalists' drive to increase profits actually leading to a declining rate of profit.[178] One way in which capitalists might think they can increase profits is to increase production. However, since each capitalist is driven to do this or risk going out of business, a crisis of 'overproduction' emerges. With more goods being made than capitalists can sell, they try to reduce workers' wages or indeed sack workers, which in turn unleashes a cascade as fewer goods can be sold and in turn bosses sack more workers. In short, capitalists try to increase their profits by increasing production but this has the unintended consequence of leading to a crisis of overproduction where less profit is made.[179]

The unintended consequences of actions is not the only way Marx's thinking about the dialectic differs from Hegel's. Hegel held that our thinking should make no assumptions or presuppositions; however, Marx does not hold that science must be presuppositionless. As Murray agues:

> Marx does not leave the circle of Hegelian systematic dialectics unbroken: he objects to the 'presuppositionlessness' of Hegelian systematic dialectics and insists that science has premises, which he and Engels sketched in *The German Ideology*. The premises are given by nature and are not themselves subject to being incorporated as 'results' of some more cosmic systematic dialectic, reappear in *Capital* and testify to Marx's explicit and frequently reaffirmed divergence from strictly Hegelian systematic dialectics (at least as he, questionably, understood Hegel).[180]

Ignoring Murray's aside that Marx misunderstood Hegel, Murray's main point seems well put. In fact, Callinicos argues that one could go further and claim that "Marx's theory presupposes, not just nature, but all the relations and mechanisms it posits as existing independently as the real 'premises' of his theory".[181]

Engels and the 'Laws of the Dialectics'

If someone knew only one thing about dialectics, it would possibly be that according to Engels there were three laws of the dialectics. Writing in the *Dialectics of Nature* he argues:

> It is, therefore, from the history of nature and human society that the laws of dialectics are abstracted. For they are nothing but the most general laws of these two

aspects of historical development, as well as of thought itself. And indeed they can be reduced in the main to three:

The law of the transformation of quantity into quality and vice versa;

The law of the interpenetration of opposites;

The law of the negation of the negation.

All three are developed by Hegel in his idealist fashion as mere laws of *thought*: the first, in the first part of his *Logic*, in the Doctrine of Being; the second fills the whole of the second and by far the most important part of his *Logic*, the Doctrine of Essence; finally the third figures as the fundamental law for the construction of the whole system.[182]

A preliminary point to make here is that it is Engels not Hegel who is claiming that dialectics can in the main be reduced to three so-called laws. We can find nowhere in Hegel's writings where he makes such a claim.[183]

We wish to argue that Engels' second law, the interpenetration of opposites, is actually an amalgam of what Hegel describes as the first and second sides of his dialectic: the 'understanding' and the dialectical or negatively rational side. It will be remembered that the 'understanding' views objects in isolation whereas the dialectical or negatively rational side sees these isolated views pass into their opposites or negations. We argued that these two sides of Hegel's dialectic are reciprocally interconnected with each constituting and requiring the other. This thought is well captured by the phrasing of Engel's second law, the interpenetration of opposites.

Engel's third law, the negation of the negation, is the third side of Hegel's dialectic, the speculative or positively rational.

In this third side there is not only a coming together of the 'understanding' and the dialectical or negatively rational side but also a resolving of the contradiction between and the transition to a new higher category. Seeing that this is the case is greatly helped by the fact that Hegel, as we have noted, sometimes refers to this third side by the phrase 'negation of the negation', which Engel's employs.

With regard to Engel's second and third laws it is clear that there is a great deal of justification for his arguing that the key aspects of Hegel's dialectic can be captured by them. This is because the second and third laws actually contain the three sides of Hegel's dialectic. However, matters are much less clear with regard to Engel's first law, the transformation of quantity into quality and vice versa. This first law refers to the claim that the accumulation of quantitative changes may, although not necessarily, at some point bring about qualitative changes and vice versa. For example, if the temperature of water is increased by 1º Celsius there will be no change in the qualitative nature or state of the water.⁴ However, if the temperature is continually raised by 1º Celsius, then when the temperature of the water reaches 100º Celsius there will be a qualitative or state change as it turns into steam.

We do not question whether others apart from Engels held that such change takes place. Engels in *Anti-Dühring* quotes Marx's *Capital* to this effect: "Here, as in natural science, is shown the correctness of the law discovered by Hegel in his *Logic*, that merely quantitative changes beyond a certain point pass into qualitative differences".[184] Nor do we doubt that such changes take place, in fact they appear common. We also do not to deny that Hegel is concerned with both quantity and quality, both of which he discusses at some length in the *Science of Logic* and *The Encyclopaedia Logic*. Moreover, Hegel does point out that thinking about quality leads to the thought of quantity, and that the thought of quantity leads back to quality. Rather our doubt

4 Unless of course the water is already at a temperature of 99º Celsius

is whether the first law actually captures something central to Hegel's dialectics to the same degree as the second and third laws do.

What did Marx Learn from Hegel?

In conclusion, we have argued that Marx (and Engels) learnt a number of important things from Hegel regarding dialectics, with the most important being the central place that dialectics should have in our thinking. This is, firstly, because as Engels notes in *Socialism: Utopian and Scientific:* "For the first time the whole world, natural, historical, intellectual, is represented as a process, i.e., as in constant motion, change, transformation, development; and the attempt is made to trace out the internal connection that makes a continuous whole of all this movement and development".[185] Secondly, that the outcome of the dialectic is not simply a combination of what has gone before but instead the dialectic produces something that is new in some strong sense. Thirdly, it is the dialectic that drives history forward as a result of its internal contradictions.

Chapter 5
Conclusion: Hegel and Not Hegel

In writing this book we wished to provide not only an introduction to the thought and life of Hegel but also an outline of the very strong influence Hegel had on Marx and Engels. This latter point is important because Hegel's philosophy is one of the three main sources of Marxism and outside of academic philosophical circles it is principally through this current that Hegel continues to exert an influence on contemporary life.

Three Sources and Three Component Parts of Marxism
Vladimir Ilyich Lenin, one of the leaders of the Russian Revolution, argued that Marxism "is the legitimate successor to the best that man produced in the nineteenth century, as represented by German philosophy, English political economy and French socialism".[186]

By 'French socialism' Lenin had in mind that the French Revolution had "revealed the *struggle of classes* as the basis and the driving force of all development".[187] For those involved in the fight against the worst excesses of capitalism and the battle to reform or even overthrow it, 'the struggle of classes' seems to be the most familiar and well-known of these three sources and components, although this does not mean that it is straightforward.

Lenin is alluding to the work of Adam Smith and David Ricardo in his reference to 'English political economy'. Their key insight, Lenin correctly argues, was to lay the foundations for Marx to develop the *labour theory of value* which holds, roughly, that the value of a commodity depends on the relative quantity of labour which is necessary for its production.[188] However, matters here are not straightforward. For, on the one hand, it is true that Marx gave his most thought to economics, leaving us an unmatched if unfinished account of capitalism and how it developed. "Having recognised that the economic system is the foundation on which the political superstructure is erected,

Marx devoted most of his attention to the study of this economic system. Marx's principal work, *Capital*, is devoted to a study of the economic system of modern, i.e., capitalist, society".[189] Yet, on the other, unfortunately, mainstream economic thought often seems so far divorced from reality and Marx's insight that a familiarity with it appears to be of little worth in understanding how the world actually works. (Of course, the world is not divided neatly into politics on the one hand and economics on the other, despite the best efforts of the media, politicians and many academics to tell us so.)

But what of the third element — German philosophy? Matters here are even less straightforward. By 'German philosophy' Lenin means in the main the thought of Hegel. Lenin argued that Marx "developed philosophy to a higher level, he enriched it with the achievements of German classical philosophy, especially of Hegel's system".[190] However, philosophy of any sort is rarely taught in schools and is increasingly at the margins of universities. Further, it only infrequently features in the popular media. Given this, socialists may be less familiar with this third element of Marxism. There are resources to help us understand philosophy. For example, John Molyneux's recent *The Point is to Change It*[191] is an engaging introduction to Marxist philosophy.

A Helping Hand from Hegel

After having read this short book we hope you will agree with us that an understanding of Hegel's thought is useful in understanding capitalism and, more importantly, the fight against it. We are not alone in holding that this is the case. Let us return to Lenin again. "It is impossible completely to understand Marx's *Capital*, and especially its first chapter, without having thoroughly studied and understood the whole of Hegel's *Logic*. Consequently, half a century later none of the Marxists understood Marx!"[192] We should make it clear that Lenin's comments tend here towards hyperbole, but the key point to take away is the fact that Marx's greatest work, *Capital*, is profoundly influenced by Hegel's most important one, *Logic*.[193] And you do not have to take Lenin's word for it either. In 1858 as Marx was writing *Grundrisse* — held by many to be the first draft of *Capital* or at least a plan for it — he wrote a letter to Engels stating:

> What was of great use to me as regard method of treatment was Hegel's *Logic* at which I had taken another look by mere accident... If ever the time comes when such work is again possible, I should very much like to write 2 or 3 sheets making accessible to the common reader the rational aspect of the method which Hegel not only discovered but also mystified.[194]

Marx never did have the time to write those two or three sheets. However, our outline of Hegel's method and our account of the way it was 'mystified' provides an idea of how Hegel's method proved so valuable for Marx.

Some Trouble with Non-Hegelian Marxism

Hegel has been seen by some as an unhelpful influence upon Marxism. Further, they have tried to alter Marxism in a non-Hegelian direction. However, it is our belief that this is a terrible mistake and that it has had awful consequences. This is shown perhaps most clearly via the influence of the 'mechanical

Marxism' of Stalin, which sought to exclude key aspects of Hegel's thought,[195] the most important of which was that Hegel was insistent about the centrality of human agency; that is, it is human beings that bring about change.

Marx had pointed out that it is human beings who "make their own history".[196] Like Hegel, Marx rejected the idea that history exists as an independent force carrying us along in its wake. In contrast, the Marxism of Stalin's Russia claimed that socialism was inevitable and not something that had to be fought for and won by human beings. Such 'mechanical Marxism' undermined Marx's insistence that socialism which is "the emancipation of the working class is the act of the working class".[197] Plekhanov, who is often considered to be the father of Russian Marxism, expressed this mechanical tendency most clearly when he wrote: "We, indeed, know our way and are seated in that historical train which at full speed takes us to our goal... [The historical process is] going to its logical conclusion with the unswerving character of astronomical phenomena".[198] Thus, mechanical Marxism argues that slavery was replaced by feudalism, which was replaced by capitalism which, inevitably, will be replaced by socialism. But it is simply mistaken to hold that there is anything fatalistic about these changes.

A practical example of the danger of mechanical Marxism was seen in the 1930s and 1940s. At that time, fascism in Europe represented the largest danger that the working class has perhaps ever encountered. Fascism, for mechanical Marxism, was a brief deviation from the general upwards path of historical 'progress' and this analysis led the German Communist Party to argue that any victory for Hitler would be short-lived. This lay behind the 'third period' policy of the Communist International or Comintern. Directed by Stalin, the Comintern proclaimed that capitalism was entering a period of final collapse and social democratic parties were in fact 'social fascists', that is, a version of fascism. Consequently, it argued that not only should communist parties not work with social democratic parties against the fascists, but they should do their utmost to destroy them. The rise of Mussolini, Franco and, most terribly, Hitler shows the tragedy of what non-Hegelian Marxism can result in. In short, if the crucial Hegelian insight that humans create history is removed from Marxism, a fatalism ensues which can result in the most tragic misunderstanding of what is to be done.

To be clear here we are not arguing that the mechanical Marxism of Stalinism and the subsequent rise of fascism was the result of Stalin not reading enough Hegel! The prominence of mechanical Marxism was rather a theoretical justification for actions taken for economic and/or political reasons. Having said this, a clearer grasp of the centrality of Hegel's thought for a Marxist understanding of the world may have made it easier to see the errors of mechanical Marxism and to oppose the distortions and false claims to orthodoxy of Stalinism and its policies.

The shortcomings of mechanical Marxism and the attempt to excise the influence of Hegel from Marxist thinking continued after World War II. One of the most important post-war Marxist theorists was Louis Althusser. Althusser was a long-time member — although sometimes a strong critic — of the French Communist Party. In his early life he held that Marxism was, of necessity, Hegelian in that it aimed at human flourishing. However, in 1950 Althusser revised this view when he argued that the post-war mania for Hegel in France was only a bourgeois attempt to combat Marx as the originator of a philosophy totally distinct from Hegel's.[199]

On the basis of his new reading of Marx, Althusser argued that not only was Marx the originator of a new philosophy, dialectical materialism, that had nothing to do with its Hegelian and Feuerbachian precursors, but also that Marx had founded a new science, historical materialism, which broke with and superseded such ideological and pre-scientific precursors as the political economics of Smith and Ricardo. Althusser's version of Marxism is a beguilingly complex one that removes, or at least reduces, the role of human agency in changing the world. Rather than men and women making history, history is made by the positions that human have inside structures within society. Further, historical materialism was, in the first instance, an epistemology, a theory of knowledge not a guide to action. Finally, this epistemology, what Althusser called 'theoretical practice', takes place entirely within thought. In short, we would argue that Althusser's non-Hegelian Marxism strips away the very heart of Marxism, the attempt to fight for a better world.

Some trouble with Reading Hegel

A problem with appreciating the importance of Hegel is the way he writes.   Arthur Schopenhauer, who was a colleague of Hegel, claimed that:

> the greatest effrontery in serving up sheer nonsense, in scrabbling together senseless and maddening webs of words, such as had previously been heard in madhouses, finally appeared in Hegel. It became the instrument of the most ponderous and general mystification that has ever existed, with a result that will seem incredible to posterity, and be a lasting monument of German stupidity.[200]

Further, Beiser — who is very sympathetic to Hegel — holds that: "Reading Hegel is often a trying and exhausting experience, the intellectual equivalent of chewing gravel".[201]

Indeed it is arguable that some of Hegel's writings are amongst the most difficult of philosophical texts, ranking alongside the works of Aristotle (which in the main are short-hand lecture notes written by students some 2,500 years ago) and Kant's *Critique of Pure Reason*.

We have quoted Hegel at some length and chosen passages that are most clear and easily intelligible, but to gently remind you of just how difficult he can be to read, here is a typical example from *The Phenomenology of Spirit:*

While qua consciousness, it no doubt comes outside itself, still, in being outside itself, it is at the same time restrained within itself, it exists for itself, and its self-externalization is for consciousness. Consciousness finds that it immediately is and is not another consciousness, as also that this other is for itself only when it cancels itself as existing for itself.[202]

Excuses can be made. Conventional language encourages us to think of a table as a table, not something that, in Hegel's terms, is in a process of becoming (from a tree trunk before, to a ground-up mass of woodchips in the recycling plant), or something that is only a table when it has a relation to its user as a supporting surface.

For this reason Hegel very often found it very difficult to express his ideas in an accessible way through written language, and nothing can change that.

Some Trouble with What Marx Learnt from Hegel

It should perhaps come as no surprise that, more than 10 years into the Great Recession which began with the financial crash of 2008, there has been another spike in interest in the ideas of Marx and Engels. It is however perhaps a sign of quite how dramatically the election of Jeremy Corbyn in 2015 changed the Labour Party that John McDonnell, his Shadow Chancellor, was happy to acknowledge that "there's a lot to learn from reading *Das Kapital*".[203]

Perhaps it is more surprising that there has also been a resurgence in interest in the influence of Hegel on Marx. For example, one sign of this is that in the last few years alone a number of books have been published in English on this matter.[204]

Callinicos argues that "Increasingly the question of the Marx-Hegel relationship has come to focus on the extent to which the system of categories that Hegel elaborates in the *Logic* influenced Marx's conceptual construction".[205] Callinicos is critical of this trend and we agree with him. Moreover, this seems to us to be a great shame as it is far too narrow a basis on which to assess just what Marx did learn from Hegel. It is too narrow in at least two ways.

The first is that whilst Hegel's the *Science of Logic* is seen by many as the most important of his works, Hegel was arguably the philosopher who developed the most all-encompassing of philosophical systems, and to focus on but one of his works will necessarily narrow the assessment of his influence.

This is particularly the case given the fact that the *Science of Logic* contains little or nothing of his account of the philosophy of history (see *Lectures on the Philosophy of World History: Introduction*), alienation (see *Phenomenology of Spirit*) or the state (see *Philosophy of Right*). Similarly, only considering Marx's conceptual construction as the basis to assess Hegel's influence on him would seem to be as far as one could get from the central issues that occupied this lifelong revolutionary.

Towards a Conclusion

Despite the centrality of Hegel to Marx's thought, from the point of view of the twenty-first century with its economic inequalities, looming environmental disaster, imperialism, rising racism and a host of other pressing issues, looking back at Hegel might appear to be an exercise with little worth.

When surveys find that British people are more likely to believe in ghosts than a creator, and just 55 per cent of self-identified Christians believe in God, there seems to be little place for Hegel's Absolute Spirit.[206]

So in many respects he appears walled off from us, not only through the passage of time, but because his ideas seemingly have no modern echo and at best are the province of a tiny minority of academic philosophers.

Even on the left it might be assumed that whatever significance there once was for Hegel, he was superseded by Marx and there is little if anything that remains of his influence on contemporary Marxist thought, leaving him of antiquarian interest or a historical footnote at best.

We hope this brief introduction to his work has done something to dispel that impression. There is a fresh and exciting quality about Hegel that derives from a way of seeing the world which is dynamic, restless and subversive of the norm. Hegel may be writing about the Prussian state, a monarch, or the Church, but to him all of these are related to everything else and are themselves affected by this relationship. So they are not just the Prussian state, a monarch or empire but something more. At the same time, they are moving forward in time, becoming something that they were not before and, in so doing, ceasing to be what they were. In appreciating these aspects we are not reliant on any particular conclusion that Hegel reached about the Prussian state, the monarchy or the Church.

A potter may turn out large or small pots, of different colours, and of a different shape, but the *method* of pot-making can remain essentially the same. The same consideration applies to Hegel's work. A sure sign of the distinction between Hegel's method and the varied conclusions that could result from its application was that immediately after his death in 1831 his followers split into two diametrically opposed camps: the so-called Young Hegelians and Old (or Right) Hegelians. The former (including the young Karl Marx) wanted to radically transform German society, while the latter believed that it was the embodiment of the Absolute Spirit and the *status quo* must not be challenged.

It could be argued that such schisms are common. For example, the followers of Marx divided into the revolutionaries and reformists, while the followers of Lenin divided into Stalinists and Trotskyists. However, in these latter cases the splits were driven by real world events.

It took 34 years for the Third International to emerge and rival the Second, and this was tied to the gradual integration of former revolutionaries into capitalist society (through parliament and trade union activity). The divisions in Russia developed quickly but were driven by the critical situation of isolation the Bolshevik Party found itself in. Stalinism was not inherent in Leninism but a repudiation of it. However, the split into Young and Old Hegelians was inherent in Hegel's thinking alone. Indeed, in many respects he had lived that split himself. The radical youth and the reactionary establishment figure were but phases of a life during which he expounded a single system that remained relatively consistent over time.

We cannot know what Hegel would have made of the Young/Old Hegelian controversy, but strip away the specific points he made, which in many cases can be inaccurate, out-of-date, or plain reactionary, and we are still left with a philosophical approach that achieves a better grasp of the complexities of change, and a deeper understanding of the world, than the formalist thinkers of capitalism or Stalinism could ever hope for. And so, for all that one of Hegel's great innovations was to put a sense of history into the study of philosophy, in one sense his work is timeless.

If we apply his concepts of becoming and of the inter-relatedness of things it becomes clear, as we hope we have shown, that his thought remains very influential on a Marxist understanding of the world. The starting point is not G. W. F. Hegel (1770–1831) but a body of thought and writings that occupy a point in time between the transformative impact of the French Revolution and the birth of the modern labour movement.

Furthermore, the process of becoming did not start in 1770 and nor did it end in 1831. Hegel's thought had an impact on others. It had a relation to other philosophers that stretched backwards (in its formative stages) and drove forwards at the same time. So Hegel worked on and transformed ideas out of the material given to him, both culturally (such as previous philosophers like Kant) and through historical events such as the 1789 revolution.

Those that followed — particularly Marx and Engels — used his thought in exactly the same dynamic way. They did so because in their work Hegel is stood on his head, and to that extent fundamentally broken with. In Marxism, therefore, we have the thought of Hegel and not Hegel all at the same time.

This is good news. While it is a commendable and worthwhile exercise to read works such as *The Phenomenology of Spirit,* and we certainly would not want to dissuade you from that, it is not necessary to metaphorically chew gravel in order to come into contact with the Hegelian method. It suffuses the writings of Marx, Engels, Lenin and other Marxists.

Yet there is more to be said. Marx's writings — written as they were between 1842 and 1883 — are also products of their time and so in some instances are inevitably 'out-of-date'. Lenin, on the hundredth anniversary of the 1917 Russian revolution, was almost totally ignored in Russia. But it is legitimate to talk about Marxism and Leninism as contemporary currents because what Marx wrote about Louis Bonaparte or Lenin wrote about the development of capitalism in Russia reflect an application of a method tied to living forces in society today: the working class and the oppressed on the one hand and their class enemies, capitalism and imperialism, on the other.

With a world in crisis at so many levels, and with threats to humanity's very existence growing all the time, everyone who tries to understand this reality in all its inter-connected complexity, and who seeks radical action to change it for the better, owes, like Marx, an enormous debt to Hegel.

Further Reading

The best short introduction to Hegel and his thought is Peter Singer's (1983) *Hegel: A Very Short Introduction* (Oxford University Press) whilst Frederick Beiser's (2005) *Hegel* (Routledge) is the most accessible full book-length presentation.

Arguably the best biography of Hegel is Terry Pinkard's (2000) *Hegel: A Biography* (Cambridge University Press), though at over 800 pages it is by no means a short read.

John W. Burbidge's (2006) *The Logic of Hegel's Logic* (Broadview Press) really is an excellent guide to Hegel's 'logic' as presented in both the *Science of Logic* and *Encyclopaedia Logic*. It has the added virtue of being short.

Joseph McCarney's (2000) *Hegel on History* (Routledge) cannot be recommended enough as it is a wonderfully clear and accessible (with some work) guide to Hegel's thought on the philosophy of history.

If you've been bitten by the Hegel bug then Frederick Beiser's (2006) *Cambridge Companion to Hegel* (Cambridge University Press) contains a host of excellent academic articles that (with quite a lot of work) help deepen one's understanding of Hegel.

Finally, Michael Inwood's (1992) *A Hegel Dictionary* (Blackwell) does a really useful job of providing a linguist, historical and philosophical analysis of many of the key terms that Hegel uses.

Bibliography

The works of Hegel listed below will generally be acknowledged as the standard translations. The Marxist Internet Archive (https://www.marxists.org/) hosts all of Marx and Engels' works that we refer to. However, typically below we reference printed versions of these work as we believe that these allow the reader to mark and annotate them as well as more easily re-read and revisit them.

Althusser, Louis (1950) 'Le retour à Hegel. Dernier mot du révisionisme universitaire', *La Nouvelle Critique,* 20, translated as 'The Return of Hegel: The Latest Word in Academic Revisionism' by G. M. Goshgarian (1997) in *The Spectre of Hegel: Early Writings* (Verso).

Andrew, Edward (1983) 'Class in Itself and Class Against Capital: Karl Marx and his Classifiers' in *Canadian Journal of Political Science,* XVI: 3, p. 577.

Beiser, Frederick (1993) 'Hegel's Historicism' in *The Cambridge Companion to Hegel* edited by Frederick C. Beiser (Cambridge University Press).

Beiser, Frederick (2005) *Hegel* (Routledge).

Beiser, Frederick (2006) *Cambridge Companion to Hegel* (Cambridge University Press).

Burbidge, John W. (2006) *The Logic of Hegel's Logic* (Broadview).

Callinicos, Alex (1983) *The Revolutionary Ideas of Karl Marx* (Bookmarks).

Callinicos, Alex (2014) *Deciphering Capital Deciphering Capital: Marx's Capital and its Destiny* (Bookmarks).

Cartwright, Nancy (1983) *How the Laws of Physics Lie* (Oxford University Press).

Collingwood, R. G. (1946) *The Idea of History* (Oxford University Press).

Dogan, Sevgi (2018) *Marx and Hegel on the Dialectic of the Individual and the Social* (Lexington Books).

Engels, Friedrich (1845/1993) *The Condition of the English Working Class* (Oxford University Press).

Engels, Friedrich (1886/1996) *Ludwig Feuerbach and the End of Classical German Philosophy* (J. H. W. Dietz).

Engels, Friedrich (1892) *Socialism: Utopian and Scientific* in Robert Tucker (ed.) (1978) *The Marx-Engels Reader,* second edition (Norton).

Engels, Friedrich (1954a) *Dialectics of Nature,* second edition (Progress Publishers).

Engels, Friedrich (1954b) *Anti-Dühring* (Progress Publishers).

Fareld, Victoria and Hanned Kuch (eds) (2019) *From Marx to Hegel and Back: Capitalism, Critique, and Utopia Hardcover* (Bloomsbury Academic).

Feuerbach, Ludwig (1844) *The Essence of Christianity* translated from the second German edition by Marian Evans (John Chapman).

Findlay, J. L. (1958) *Hegel: A Re-examination* (George Allen and Unwin).

Forster, Michael (1993) 'Hegel's Dialectical Method' in Frederick C. Beiser (ed.) *The Cambridge Companion to Hegel* (Cambridge University Press).

Fukuyama, F. (1992) *The End of History and the Last Man* (Penguin).

Gooch, G. P. (1924/2012) *Germany and the French Revolution* (Forgotten Books).

Hegel, G. W. F. (1807/1977) *Phenomenology of Spirit,* translated by A. V. Miller with analysis of the text and foreword by J. N. Findlay (Oxford University Press).

Hegel, G. W. F. (1812–16/1989) *Science of Logic* translated by A. V. Miller with a foreword by J. N. Findlay (Humanity Books).

Hegel, G. W. F. (1821/1952) *Philosophy of*

Right translated by T. M. Knox (Oxford University Press).

Hegel, G. W. F. (1830/1971) *Hegel's Philosophy of Mind* translated by W. Wallace and revised by A. V. Miller (Oxford University Press). This is a translation of the third volume of Hegel's *Encyclopaedia*.

Hegel, G. W. F. (1830/1991) *The Encyclopaedia Logic* (with the Zusätze), translated by T. F. Geraets, W. A. Suchting and H. S. Harris (Hackett Publishing). This is a translation of the first volume of Hegel's *Encyclopaedia*.

Hegel, G. W. F. (1830/1956) *The Philosophy of History*, translated by J. Sibree with an introduction by C. J. Friedrich (Dover Philosophical Classics).

Hegel, G. W. F. (1970) *On Art, Religion and Philosophy* edited by J. Glenn Gray (New York).

Hegel, G. W. F. (1975) *Lectures on the Philosophy of History. Introduction: Reason in History*, translated by H. B. Nisbet with an introduction by D. Forbes (Cambridge University Press).

Hegel, G. W. F. (1830/1991) *The Philosophy of History* (Prometheus Books).

Hegel, G. W. F. (2008) *Outlines of the Philosophy of Right* (Oxford University Press).

Hegel, G.W. F. (1807/2016) *The Phenomenology of Spirit* (Pantianos Classics).

Houlgate, Stephen (1998) *An Introduction to Hegel: Freedom, Truth and History*, second edition (Blackwell).

Inwood, Michael (1992) *A Hegel Dictionary* (Blackwell).

Kant, Immanuel (1781 & 1787/1956) *The Critique of Practical Reason*, translated by Lewis Beck White (Bobbs-Merrill).

Kant, Immanuel (1787/1996) *Critique of Pure Reason*, translated by Werner S. Pluher (Hackett Publishing).

Kant, Immanuel (1991) *Political Writings*, translated by H. B. Nisbet (Cambridge University Press).

Kojeve, Alexandre (1980) *Introduction to the Reading of Hegel* translated by J. H. Nichols (Cornell University Press).

Lenin, Vladimir Ilyich (1913) 'The Three Sources and Three Component Parts of Marxism' reproduced in Robert T. Tucker (1975) *The Lenin Anthology* (Norton).

Lenin, Vladimir Ilyich (1929) *Conspectus of Hegel's Science of Logic: Book III (Subjective Logic or the Doctrine of the Notion)* at: https://www.marxists. org/archive/lenin/works/1914/cons-logic/ch03.htm

Lovato, Brian C. (2017) *Democracy, Dialectics, and Difference: Hegel, Marx, and 21st Century Social Movements* (Routledge).

Lukács, Georg (1975) The *Young Hegel: Studies in the Relations between Dialectics and Economics* translated by Rodney Livingstone (Merlin Press).

Maker, William (2000) 'The Science of Freedom: Hegel's Critical Theory' in *Hegel Bulletin*, Vol. 21, Issue 1–2, No. 41/42 at: https://www.cambridge. org/core/journals/hegel-bulletin/ article/science-of-freedom-hegels-critical-theory/32D9ADA0088A570D7 F86AF9C31E85F3B

Marx, Karl (1844) *Economic and Philosophic Manuscripts of 1844* in Tucker (ed.) (1978) *The Marx-Engels Reader*, second edition (Norton).

Marx, Karl (1847/1956) *The Poverty of Philosophy* (Foreign Languages Publishing House).

Marx, Karl (1852) *The Eighteenth Brumaire of Louis Bonaparte* in Tucker (ed.) (1978) *The Marx-Engels Reader*, second edition (Norton).

Marx, Karl (1859) Preface to *A Contribution to the Critique of Political Economy* in Tucker (ed.) (1978) *The Marx-Engels Reader*, second edition (Norton).

Marx, Karl (1864) 'General Rules of the International Workingmen's Association', http://www.marxists. org/history/international/iwma/ documents/1864/rules.htm

Marx, Karl (1867/1976) *Capital*, Volume 1 (Penguin).

Marx, Karl (1875) *Critique of the Gotha Programme* at: https://www.marxists. org/archive/marx/works/1875/ gotha/ch01.htm

Marx, Karl (1888) *Theses on Feuerbach* in Tucker (ed.) (1978) *The Marx-Engels Reader*, second edition (Norton).

Marx, Karl (1992) *Capital*, Volume 3 (Penguin Classics).

Marx, Karl (1993) *Grundrisse: Foundations of the Critique of Political Economy*

(Penguin Classics).

Marx, Karl and Friedrich Engels (1848) *The Manifesto of the Communist Party* in Tucker (ed.) (1978) *The Marx-Engels Reader*, second edition (Norton).

Marx, Karl and Friedrich Engels (1974) *The German Ideology*, student edition, second edition, edited and introduced by C. J. Arthur (Lawrence and Wishart).

Marx, Karl and Friedrich Engels (1983) *Karl Marx and Friedrich Engels Collected Works* (Lawrence and Wishart).

Maybee, Julie E. (2016) 'Hegel's Dialectics', *The Stanford Encyclopaedia of Philosophy* (winter edition), Edward N. Zalta (ed.) at: https://plato.stanford.edu/archives/win2016/entries/hegel-dialectics/

McCarney, Joseph (2000) *Hegel on History* (London).

Meszaros, Istvan (2005) *Marx's Theory of Alienation*, fifth edition (Merlin).

Molyneux, John (2012) *The Point is to Change It* (Bookmarks).

Murray, Patrick (2000) 'Marx's "Truly Social" Labour Theory of Value: Part I', *Historical Materialism*, 7, p. 27–65.

Nietzsche, Frederick (1980) *On the Advantage and Disadvantage of History for Life*, translated by P. Preuss (Hackett Publishing).

Norman, Richard (1976) *Hegel's Phenomenology* (Sussex University Press).

Olende, Ken (forthcoming) 'Marxism and Race: A Centric Analysis', *International Socialism*.

Pinkard, Terry (2000) *Hegel. A Biography* (Cambridge University Press).

Plato (1961) *The Collected Dialogues of Plato* edited by Edith Hamilton and Huntington Cairns (Princeton University Press).

Plekhanov, G. V. (1905) *Socialism and Political Struggle* (Geneva) quoted in

Arthur P. Mendel (1961): *Dilemmas of Progress in Tsarist Russia: Legal Marxism and Legal Populism* (Harvard University Press).

Novack, George (1978) *Polemics in Marxist Philosophy* (Pathfinder Press).

Popper, Karl (1963) *Conjectures and Refutations* (Basic Books).

Said, Edward (1973) *Orientalism* (Penguin Books).

Schopenhauer, A. (1819 and 1844/1969) *The World as Will and Representation*, two volumes (Dover Publications).

Sherry, Dave (2017) *Russia 1917: Workers' Revolution and the Festival of the Oppressed* (Bookmarks).

Smith, Adam (1978) *Lectures on Jurisprudence* edited by R. Meek, D. Raphael, and P. Stein (Clarendon Press).

Singer, Peter (1983) *Hegel: A Very Short Introduction* (Oxford University Press).

Solomon, Robert (1983) *In the Spirit of Hegel: A Study of G. W. F. Hegel's 'Phenomenology of Spirit'* (Oxford University Press).

Stace, W.T. (1924/1955) *The Philosophy of Hegel: A Systematic Exposition* (Dover Publications).

Stone, Alison (2017) 'Hegel and Colonialism', *Hegel Bulletin*, pp. 1–24.

Sullivan, Terence (2001) 'The Lewontin Test', *Radical Philosophy*, 110 (November/December).

Swain, D. (2012) *Alienation: An Introduction to Marx's Theory* (Bookmarks).

Taylor, Charles (1979) *Hegel and Modern Society* (Cambridge University Press).

Tucker, Robert (ed.) (1978) *The Marx-Engels Reader*, second edition (Norton).

Uchida, Hiroshi and Terrell Carver (2016) *Marx's 'Grundrisse' and Hegel's 'Logic'* (Routledge).

Wilkins, B. T. (1974) *Hegel's Philosophy of History* (Cornell University Press).

Notes

1   Spirit is one way to translate the German word 'geist'. Another common way is as 'mind'. The *Phenomenology of Spirit* is sometimes referred to as the *Phenomenology of Mind*, but in allowing for a more cultural sense, as in the phrase 'spirit of the age' ('Zeitgeist'), the former seems a more suitable rendering for the title. It is also the more common rendering and we will use it here. The *Phenomenology of Spirit* was Hegel's first major work and it is widely seen to be an introduction to the whole of his philosophical system (Hegel, 1807/1977).

2   Pastor Ewald quoted in Gooch, 1924/2012, p. 371.

3   Quoted in Lukács, 1975, p. 138.

4   Quoted in Lukács, 1975, p. 132.

5   Quoted in Lukács, 1975, p. 131.

6   Quoted in Lukács, 1975, p. 46.

7   Quoted in Lukács, 1975, p. 46.

8   Quoted in Lukács, 1975, p. 454.

9   Quoted in Pinkard, 2000, p. 451.

10   Hegel, 2016, p. 165.

11   Hegel, 2016, p. 166.

12   Gooch, 1924/2012, p. 285.

13   Gooch, 1924/2012, p. 56.

14   Hegel, 2016, p. 6.

15   Hegel, 2016, p. 6.

16   Hegel, 1830/1991 https://www.marxists.org/reference/archive/hegel/works/sl/slappear.htm

17   Hegel, 2016, pp. 8–9.

18   See Pinkard, 2000, pp. 30–33.

19   See Pinkard, 2000, p. 200.

20   Pinkard, 2000, p. 228.

21   Quoted in Lukács, 1975, p. 452.

22   We take the phrase 'world soul' to be a more poetic way (or perhaps simply a different way) to translate 'world historical figure' which we discuss at length in Chapter 3.

23   Lukács, 1975, p. 462.

24   Quoted in Maker, 2000.

25   Quoted in Lukács, 1975, p. 506.

26   Hegel, 2008, p. 16.

27   Hegel, 2008, p. 14. This edition says: "What is actual is rational and what is rational is actual."

28   Quoted in Lukács, 1975, p. 459.

29   Hegel, 2008, p. 229.

30   Hegel, 1821/1952, pp. 444–5.

31   Hegel, 1821/1952, p. 456.

32   Hegel, 1821/1952, p. 456.

33   Hegel, 1821/1952, p. 473.

34   Hegel, 1807/1977, p. 50.

35   Michael Inwood (1992) argues that Hegel uses spirit in no less than nine different ways, viewing these not as nine distinct senses of spirit but rather as related phases that are systematically related in the development of a single spirit.

36   Hegel, 1807/1977, p. 294, emphasis in the original.

37   Hegel, 1807/1977, p. 294. Hegel's talk of the self-consciousness of the Spirit may seem strange to the modern ear. However, we want to argue that in fact many readers will already have a good understanding of it in virtue of their knowledge of another type of consciousness, namely, class consciousness.

38   Norman, 1976, and Taylor, 1979.

39   Norman, 1976, p. 88.

40   Taylor, 1979, p. 90.

41   Hegel, 1807/1977, p. 213.

42   Taylor, 1979, p. 90.

43   Taylor, 1979, p. 90.

44   Hegel, 1807/1977, p. 303.

45   Hegel, 1807/1977, p. 307.

46   Hegel, 1807/1977, p. 320.

47   Engels, 1886, p. 364. Alex Callinicos appears to agree with Engels, writing that for Hegel "Nature, as the sphere where Idea is alienated" (Callinicos, 2014, p. 114).

48   Marx, 1844, in Tucker (ed.) 1978, p. 110, emphases in the original.

49   Hegel, 1821/1952, p. 222.

50   Beiser, 2005, p. 313.

51   Feuerbach, 1844, p. 228, emphasis in the original.

52 Feuerbach, 1844, p. 228.

53 Feuerbach, 1844, p. 228.

54 As we shall argue in more depth in Chapter 3, although Marx wrote in *Capital*, Volume 1, that Hegel's philosophy was stood on its head, it was Feuerbach some decades earlier who first did the righting.

55 Engels, 1866/1996, p. 18, our emphasis.

56 For a short but clear discussion on the impact of Feuerbach on Marx's thought see Callinicos, 1983, and for a more focused assessment on alienation see Swain, 2012. The latter is also a useful introduction to Marx's account of alienation more generally.

57 Marx, 1844, in Tucker (ed.) 1978, p. 112, emphases in the original. Marx holds that another of such achievements is that "Hegel conceives the self-genesis of man as a process" (Marx in Tucker, ed., 1978, p. 110). That is, human beings create the world around them not from scratch but on the basis of what previous generations have created and, of course, destroyed. In short, human beings and the societies they create have a history.

58 Marx, 1844, in Tucker (ed.) 1978, p. 110.

59 Marx, 1844, in Tucker (ed.) 1978, p. 110, emphasis in the original.

60 Marx, 1844, in Tucker (ed.) 1978, p. 112, emphasis in the original.

61 Hegel, 1807/1977, p. 301, italics in the original. Interestingly, shortly after this quote Hegel explicitly talks about the class interests and how 'our leaders' will often use the general good or national interest as a cover for their own interests and lack of action. "The *being-for-itself*, the *will*, which, as will is not sacrificed, is the inner, separated Spirit of the various classes and 'estates', and this, in spite of its chatter about the *general* good, reserves to itself what suits its *own* best interest, and is inclined to make this chatter about the general good a substitute for action" (p. 307, emphases in the original).

62 Marx and Engels, 1974, p. 48. Animals also labour to meet their needs but human labour is distinguished by the fact that we do so consciously. "A spider conducts operations which resemble those of the weaver, and a bee would put many a human architect to shame by the construction of its honeycomb cells. But what distinguishes the worst architect from the best of bees is that the architect builds the cell in his mind before he constructs it in wax. At the end of the labour process, a result emerges which had already been conceived by the worker at the beginning..." (Marx, 1867/1976, p. 284.

63 Marx, 1844, in Tucker (ed.) 1978, p. 76. It is interesting to note that some of Hegel's writings seem to suggest that he shares with Marx the insight that work is central to being human and that alienation may involve alienation from our own labour: "Man is realised for himself be practical activity, inasmuch as he has the impulse, in the medium which is directly given to him, to produce himself, and therein at the same time to recognise himself. This purpose he achieves by the modifications of external things upon which he impresses the seal of his inner being, and then finds repeated in them his own characteristics. Man does this in order as a free subject to strip the outer world of its stubborn foreignness, and to enjoy in the shape and fashion of things a mere external reality of himself" (Hegel, 1970, quoted in Norman, 1976, p. 53.)

64 Marx, 1844, in Tucker (ed.) 1978, p. 71.

65 Marx, 1844, in Tucker (ed.) 1978, p. 74.

66 Marx and Engels, 1974, p. 60.

67 Marx, 1888, p. 144, our emphasis.

68 Marx, 1888, p. 145.

69 Andrew, 1983, p. 577.

70 Marx, 1847/1956, p. 195.

71 Lukács, 1975, p. 540. In this translation Livingstone renders the German word 'entäusserung' as 'externalisation' which is the direct German translation; however, in Hegel's writings it is normally translated as 'alienation' and we have altered his translation to reflect this.

72 All Lukács, 1975, p. 540.

73 Marx, 1844, p. 71, emphases in the original.

74 Marx, 1844, p. 84, emphases in the original.

75 For example, a pivotal concept for Plato is that of the forms. He argued

that they were divine, indivisible and changeless. Further, Plato argued that they share the features of things in the sensible world of which they are the form, but, importantly, also cause. Put another way, ordinary things gain their properties by 'imitating' forms in which case forms somehow become independent of the sensible world. Plato most famously explains the idea of the forms in his Allegory of the Cave, as told in the *Republic*, Book VII (see Plato, 1961).

76   Hegel, 1956.
77   Hegel, 1975.
78   Wilkins, 1974, p. 18.
79   Hegel, 1975, p. 44.
80   Hegel, 1975, p. 46.
81   Hegel, 1975, p. 48.
82   Hegel, 1975, p. 54.
83   Hegel, 1975, pp. 54–5.
84   Hegel, 1830/1991, p. 288.
85   Hegel, 1975, p. 46.
86   McCarney, 2000, p. 26.
87   Hegel, 1975, p. 40.
88   Here we draw heavily on the case made by McCarney, 2000.
89   Hegel, 1975, p. 41.
90   McCarney, 2000, p. 7. However, as Beiser notes, it would be a mistake to think of Hegel as the founder of historicism; rather it was Montesquieu, Johann Georg Hamann and Johann Jakob Moser who were its 'fathers' (Beiser, 2005, p. 262).
91   Beiser, 1993, p. 270.
92   Hegel, 1975, pp. 27 and 29.
93   Hegel, 1975, p. 24.
94   Marx, 1859, p. 4.
95   We should point out that during the eighteenth and nineteenth centuries, many theorists similarly divided history into different periods. For example, Adam Smith (1978) described the economic development of human societies as a sequence of four stages: the age of hunting and gathering, that of pastoralism, that of agriculture and finally that of commerce — the latter involving among other things foreign trade and manufacturing.
96   Marx and Engels, 1848, p. 491.
97   Marx, 1875.
98   Swain, 2012, p. 20.
99   To be fair to the author in question,

he is not alone in being confused about Hegel's idealism. For example, Beiser, in what is otherwise an excellent if academic introduction to Hegel argues that "It is one of the great ironies of Hegel's philosophy of history that, though it makes ideals the governing powers of history, it is really not idealistic at all" (Besier, 2005, p. 267).
100 Marx, 1873/1976, p. 102.
101 Marx, 1873/1976, p. 103.
102 "Climate does have a certain influence, however, in that neither the torrid nor the cold region can provide a basis for human freedom or for the world-historical nations" (Hegel, 1975, p. 154).
103 In this section we again draw heavily on McCarney, 2000.
104 Hegel, 1807/1977, p. 114.
105 Hegel, 1830/1971, p. 223.
106 Kojeve, 1980, p. 43, quoted in McCarney, 2000, p. 92.
107 Hegel, 1807/1975, p. 384.
108 Hegel, 1807/1975, p. 388, italics in the original.
109 Hegel, 1830/1971, p. 172.
110 Hegel, 1975, p. 83.
111 Hegel, 1975, p. 83.
112 Hegel, 1975, p. 81.
113 Hegel, 1975, p. 83.
114 Marx, 1852, p. 595.
115 Hegel, 1975, p. 89, our emphasis.
116 Hegel, 1807/1975, p. 56.
117 Thus for instance Kant's writings on the philosophy of history may be said to postulate a cunning of nature through his assertion of the "unsocial sociability of men" (Kant, 1991, p. 44, italics in the original, quoted in McCarney, 2000, p. 123). That is, the contradiction between the inclinations of living in a society and as isolated individuals. It is the interplay between these that sets humans on a path from barbarism to culture, one wholly unintended by the barbarians.
118 Hegel, 1975, p. 53. There is in fact a long tradition in biology which argues that such talk is in fact misguided. In contemporary parlance this would be rejected by many as 'genetic determinism'. For a straightforward introduction to these issues see

Sullivan, 2001.

119 Hegel, 1975, p. 36.

120 Hegel, 1975, p. 98.

121 Hegel, 1821/1952, p. 134, emphasis added.

122 McCarney, 2000, p. 166.

123 Collingwood, 1946, p. 122.

124 Fukuyama, 1992, p. xii.

125 Hegel, 1956, pp. 103, 342 and 442, emphasis in the original.

126 Hegel, 1956, p. 104, emphasis in the original.

127 Nietzsche, 1980, p. 167.

128 This strand of decolonisation is linked to earlier projects that have also tended to accuse Marxism, of Orientalism and Eurocentricism. Edward Said (1973) popularised the first term with his book *Orientalism* which accused the West of 'othering' non-Western civilisations and ways of thought.

129 Hegel, 1991, p. 81 quoted in Stone, 2017, pp. 1–24.

130 Stone, 2017, pp. 1–24 argues that the situation is in fact more complicated than this as Hegel's conception of freedom as self-determination, she argues, has significant connections with his Eurocentrism.

131 For a convincing defence of Marx from the charge of Eurocentrism see Olende (forthcoming).

132 Hegel writes of the *Parmenides* as "the grand manner in which Plato handled the dialectic" (1830/1991, ∫81, p. 129). He continues, this time in praise of Kant, that "in modern times it has mainly been Kant who reminded people of the dialectic again and reinstated it in its place of honour" (1839/1991, ∫81, pp. 129–130). (Here "∫81" refers to the 81ˢᵗ numbered paragraph of *The Encyclopaedia Logic*. Paragraphs are indicated to allow the reader to locate the quotation even if they are using a different translation.)

133 Kant, 1787/1996.

134 For Kant, pure reason means something like 'the use of reason to gain knowledge'. This is to be contrasted with his writings on *practical* reason (see Kant, 1787/1956) which is concerned with morality or more particularly deontological ethics, the thought that what gives an action moral worth is not the outcome that is achieved by the action, but the motive that is behind the action.

135 Kant, 1787/1996, p. A 426/B 454. (There were two editions of the *Critique of Pure Reason*. The first was in 1781, known as A and the second was in 1787, known as B. It is standard to refer to both editions when quoting Kant.)

136 Kant, 1787/1996, p. A 426/B 454.

137 As John Burbidge notes, Hegel sees that "...contradiction is not the end of reasoning, but rather a clue that something is wrong, pointing toward a solution that will resolve the paradox" (2006, p. 38, footnote).

138 Hegel, 1830/1991, ∫38, p. 78.

139 Hegel, 1812–16/1989, p. 28. It is worth making a note about the *Science of Logic* (known as the 'Greater Logic') and *The Encyclopaedia Logic* (known as the 'Lesser Logic'). The three volumes of the *Science of Logic* were published between 1812 and 1816. Upon beginning lecturing at the University of Heidelberg in 1816 Hegel needed a textbook for the courses he would teach which would be more manageable for his students that the highly theoretical *Science of Logic*. So in 1817 the *Encyclopaedia of the Philosophical Sciences in Outline* was published, *The Encyclopaedia Logic* being Part I. *The Encyclopaedia Logic* is constituted by a series of compact paragraphs which provided a skeleton that was to be fleshed out in Hegel's oral presentation. The *Encyclopaedia of the Philosophical Sciences in Outline* as a whole was revised in 1827 and further amendments were made in 1830. Further, after his death in 1831, 'additions' were added based on lecture notes made by his students. Given this is not surprising if there are differences between how dialectics is presented in *Science of Logic* and *The Encyclopaedia Logic;* however, it is standardly argued that they still form a coherent whole and it is a judgement that we hold to here.

140 Hegel, 1830/1991, ∫79, p. 125.

141 We have placed the word understanding in inverted commas to show that we are referring to Hegel's

technical meaning rather than the everyday sense.

142 Hegel, 1830/1991, ∫80, p. 126.

143 Hegel, 1830/1991, ∫81, p. 128.

144 Burbidge, 2006, p. 43.

145 Hegel, 1830/1991, ∫81, p. 128, emphasis in the original.

146 Hegel, 1830/1991, ∫81, p. 129, emphasis in the original.

147 Hegel, 1812–16/1989, p. 107.

148 Hegel, 1830/1991, ∫81, p. 128.

149 Hegel, 1830/1991, ∫82, p. 131.

150 Hegel, 1812–16/1969, p. 54.

151 Hegel, 1830/1991, ∫81, p. 130.

152 Marx, 1873/1976, pp. 102–3.

153 Marx, 1873/1976, p. 103.

154 Houlgate, 1998, p. 127.

155 Novack, 1978.

156 Syllogistic logic allows inferences of one conclusion from two premises. Each premise has one term in common with the conclusion, and one term in common with the other premises.

157 Hegel, 1830/1991, ∫115, p. 180, emphasis in the original.

158 Hegel, 1830/1991, ∫115, p. 180, emphasis in the original.

159 To appreciate this point it may help to note that how the word 'logic' is used outside of philosophy is very different from how it is used inside. Outside of philosophy 'logic' refers to something like "how humans think or reason"; inside philosophy it means something like "a science of inference". We think that Hegel is concerned with the former but not the latter, so talk of him rejecting the laws of identity and of non-contradiction is beside the point and actually misconstrues what is he trying to do.

160 Popper, 1963, p. 313. It is interesting to note given his generally perceived antagonism towards the dialectic that Popper goes on to write in this same section that "It can hardly be doubted that the dialectic triad describes fairly well certain steps in the history of thought, especially certain developments of ideas and theories, and of social movements which are based on ideas or theories" (p. 313).

161 Hegel, 1812–16/1989, p. 439.

162 Beiser, 2005, p. 162, emphasis in the original.

163 Hegel, 1812–16/1989, p. 440.

164 Forster, 1993, p. 142.

165 Hegel, 1807/1977, p. 11.

166 Hegel, 1807/1977, p. 11. This is a slightly different translation from the one we use in Chapter 1.

167 In August 2018 the football manager Jose Mourinho was asked if he would still be a great manager if he did not win the Premier League title with Manchester United (the team he managed at the time). His response was "Of course. Did you never spend time reading the philosopher Hegel? He said: 'The truth is in the whole'." (https://www.bbc.co.uk/sport/football/45369322). In other words, whether or not he should be judged as a great manager is not solely on the basis of his tenure at Manchester United but on his whole career. It is perhaps a testament to the enduring strength of Hegel's thought that it is able to reach across centuries and, amongst other things, provide answers at a football manager's press conference. It is also perhaps a testament to Jose Mourinho that he is the only football manager we know of to quote Hegel in his press conference and, moreover, to do it accurately and appropriately. He may indeed be a 'special one' after all.

168 Maybee, 2016, our emphasis.

169 Stace, 1924/1955, p. 97.

170 Stace, 1924/1955, p. 286.

171 Solomon, 1983, p. 230, our emphasis.

172 Findlay, 1958, p. 74 and pp. 81–2.

173 Forster, 1993, p. 145.

174 Maybee, 2016.

175 Marx and Engels, 1974, pp. 431–2.

176 Marx and Engels, 1848, pp. 473–4, our emphasis.

177 Marx and Engels, 1848, p. 483, our emphases. It should be acknowledged, especially given our point that for Marx and Engel, unlike for Hegel, how contradictions were resolved was a contingent matter, that the quotation continues thus: "Its [the bourgeoisie's] fall and the victory of the proletariat are equally inevitable." We would argue that, despite what they write, this is not Marx's nor Engel's considered position and rather they have tended towards

hyperbole in this highly political work written when revolutions were sweeping across much of Europe. For more on this see Chapter 4.

178 Marx, 1993.

179 Marx, 1992.

180 Murray, 2000, p. 38 quoted in Callinicos, 2014, p. 120, emphasis in the original.

181 Callinicos, 2014, p. 120.

182 Engels, 1954a, p. 62.

183 In the nineteenth century there was much talk about scientific laws in nature and society. However, if laws are held to be exceptionless universal generalisations that hold necessarily (although admittedly in a sense which no one has succeeded in making properly clear), then it seems that this view of laws may be mistaken. For example, Cartwright (1983) has argued that this picture depends on an oversimplified view of the world. Our suggestion here is that we should put to one side the question of whether or not the three 'laws' of the dialectic are indeed 'laws' and take them to be claimed generalisations about the world.

184 Engels, 1954b, p. 173.

185 Engels, 1892, p. 696.

186 Lenin, 1913, pp. 6401. Engels seems to have something similar in mind when he writes that "The industrial revolution is of the same importance for England as the political revolution for France, and the philosophical revolution for Germany" (Engels, 1845/1993, p. 29).

187 Lenin 1913, p. 643, emphasis in the original.

188 For a clear and straightforward explanation of the labour theory of value see Callinicos, 1983.

189 Lenin, 1913, p. 642.

190 Lenin, 1929.

191 Molyneux, 2012.

192 Lenin, 1929.

193 To be clear, we do not claim special insight when making this assertion. For example, Callinicos in *Deciphering Capital* (2014) argues that "...Marx is heavily indebted to him [Hegel] for the conception of science he develops in *Capital*..." p. 10.

194 Marx and Engels, 1983, p. 249.

195 It is often asserted that Lenin led to Stalin and that the Russian Revolution, the first successful workers' revolution, led inevitably to totalitarian dictatorship. However, this is not at all our understanding of the situation. Stalin was not the heir to the Russian Revolution but rather its gravedigger, leading a counter-revolution that over-turned its successes. For an excellent and up-to-date account of the Russian Revolution see Sherry, 2017.

196 Marx, 1852, p. 595.

197 Marx, 1864.

198 Plekhanov, 1905, p. 104.

199 Althusser, 1950.

200 Schopenhauer, 1819 and 1844/1969, p. 429.

201 Beiser, 2005, p. 1.

202 Hegel, 1807/1977, p. 112.

203 http://www.huffingtonpost. co.uk/entry/ john-mcdonnell-marxism-andrew-marr_uk_590ef88ae4b0104c734f8caf.

204 For example Fareld and Kuch (eds) 2019; Dogan, 2018; Lovato, 2017; Uchida and Carver, 2016.

205 Callinicos, 2014, p. 20.

206 yougov.co.uk/news/2016/03/26/o-we-of-little-faith

Index